DR. CHARLES A.
MONTORIO-ARCHER

EVERYBODY
PADDLES

A LEADER'S BLUEPRINT
FOR CREATING A UNIFIED TEAM

RIVER GROVE
BOOKS

Original publication by BookBaby, New York

This edition published by River Grove Books
Austin, TX
www.rivergrovebooks.com

Distributed by River Grove Books

Design and composition by Greenleaf Book Group
Cover design by Greenleaf Book Group
Originally published: New York : BookBaby, c2012.
1. Teams in the workplace. 2. Organizational behavior. 3. Personnel management.
4. Consensus (Social sciences) I. Title.

Publisher's Cataloging-in-Publication data is available.

Hardcover ISBN: 978-1-62634-101-2

Paperback ISBN: 978-1-63299-463-9

eBook ISBN: 978-1-63299-464-6

Third Edition

To the Next Generation of Leaders . . .
Pick Up Your Paddle!

CONTENTS

~

CONTENTS

Foreword

THE BOAT

~

Peter F. Borish, President,
Computer Trading Corporation

Every once in a while, though usually infrequently, you meet someone, slap your forehead, and say, "I sure wish I had known this person well prior to today." For me, Charles Montorio-Archer is one of those people.

Given my background and passion for both early-stage start-up businesses and innovative philanthropy, I invariably have too many people requesting a meeting to ask me for something. You can imagine how refreshing it was, early into our initial lunch, for Charles to be the one offering *me* inspirational conversation, insight, and passion on a host of issues. Within a few minutes I, too, had jumped aboard the "Everybody Paddles" boat.

One of the central tenets of *Everybody Paddles* is that in an environment where each of us can be isolated yet technologically connected, a successful and balanced life requires non-digital interaction with others. An essential ingredient that just about every author who contributed to this book mentions is the inclusion of a mentor. The ingredient that is often missing from digital mentoring is emotional connectedness. This intangible is too easily turned off if the sole connection is through a power button. Needing to be responsive, responsible, and resolute with a mentor assists us in getting over the hump during the inevitable stretches of frustration or rejection.

I view engagement in philanthropy as a perfect example of the need to be physically rather than simply technologically engaged. Imagine if all you did was read grant proposals, rank them, and then allocate scarce dollars—without a site visit—to meet those in need. You could wait for the numbers to come back to try to determine if, indeed, you have made an impact. Yet wouldn't it be so much more rewarding to roll up your sleeves, take the time, and make the effort to visit the programs you intend to assist? In other words, do due diligence and be a mentor!

Of course, when you become an active participant, there is the chance of failure. Charles suggests, and I agree, that we cannot run away from failure. We must embrace and learn from it. But in isolated digital space, it is too easy to run away from failure. As I said, hitting the power switch is too easy. Virtually every successful entrepreneur has experienced what I call a "park bench day." Disappointment is to be expected when we're rejected after an interview, when we're told a business plan is not good enough for funding, or when we're passed over for promotion. After a particularly tough day, it is acceptable to go sit on a park bench and ask, "How or why am I in this situation?" But it is acceptable only for the remainder of the day! Those who learn from rejection get up off the bench and get back into the game. Others give up and feel emotionally cleansed, since the cause of their stress has been removed. However, they haven't left open the possibility of future success. The Everybody Paddles concept is a journey, not a destination. The park bench is often a resting stop along the path.

After resting, we paddle and paddle, with the assistance and support of others. The Everybody Paddles movement is an exponential function; its rate of growth accelerates as more people assist others in removing obstacles to success. Charles Montorio-Archer is on to something here. I am honored to have been invited to climb aboard.

PREFACE

When I became director of a large Brooklyn-based social service agency in 2007, I knew little about management. I was a lawyer and a lobbyist. In those roles, other people made the leadership decisions. I participated and watched, but I didn't have the final say-so. Suddenly I was in charge, and hundreds of employees looked to me to make the important decisions.

I quickly began to learn management techniques on the job. I also discovered that most managers go through the same process. Getting an MBA is nice, but it does not really prepare anyone for the realities of day-to-day, real-life actions.

As a result, I decided to find books that provided realistic guidelines for someone like me or, for that matter, any executive charged with providing leadership. But I found very little. All of the management books offered advice, but not enough seemed connected to what really happens inside an organization or an office.

That's why this book came to be written. *Everybody Paddles* examines all aspects of management, from creating the original vision to communicating it to your team, with practical guidelines based on real experiences. What I learned grew into guiding principles that have helped my agency grow and maintain its position as a model for other social service agencies throughout New York. These principles will also work for any executive in any industry.

I'm a firm believer in sharing knowledge. Management is all about identifying important issues and making the best decisions. I hope this book is useful to CEOs and other managers who are striving to be better.

Introduction

BUILDING CONSENSUS WITH THE "EVERYBODY PADDLES" CONCEPT

—⁓—

This is a book about team building and leadership. I had spent some time working on how to express these concepts in a clear, concise way when the solution came to me one day as I glanced at a magazine. I was attending a conference at the time, and at that point in the schedule we were supposed to be networking for the benefit not only of ourselves but also of our organizations. Somehow, the networking party just got out of hand. Things happen. So, I walked into a vacant room, sat down on a couch, and flipped through my phone messages. That's when I saw it: a photograph of a whitewater raft on the cover of a sporting magazine.

There were five people in the raft as the river raged on, threatening to capsize them all. They were all leaning into their oars at the same moment, however, and were executing, as if in one complete, unified movement, a turn to avoid the face of a huge rock in front of them. The water parted in a V formation, splitting into two white jet streams, and all eyes were focused on the right-hand side. The intensity of their focus got to me, as well as the sense that they were all executing that one turn in total cooperation. No one was sloughing off—unlike the conventioneers at the raucous party outside. A life-or-death turn, executed perfectly, in unison, by five people.

"Everybody Paddles" became my slogan from then on. (There's a saying in my office: "Charles is crazy. Don't get in his way when he is passionate about something!") This idea had captivated me.

A few days later I was back at the Evelyn Douglin Center for Serving People in Need (EDCSPIN), the Brooklyn non-profit organization I cofounded in 1996, where we handle about $25 million a year in services for the disabled community, and I imagined paddles everywhere—all over the walls—as a symbol of this newfound image of unity. I found a store that sold me a bunch of paddles, and the next day I started nailing them to the walls. To this day they cover the premises. A few days after that, I took a magic marker and walked around our space—a large floor in an old customs building near the Brooklyn waterfront—and started writing on the paddles: "Everyone Paddles in the Same Direction, at the Same Time, Toward the Same Goal."

I see this as a process that goes far beyond my social service agency. There's no reason it can't include individual families as well as communities, cities, states, and countries. That's because Everybody Paddles represents a pattern of growth, development, and improvement that occurs when all participants work together for a common interest.

This concept is very important today. As we all know, society is divided by economics, education, classism, ageism, gender differences, religion, and partisan politics. Despite these challenges, I believe there is opportunity for unity because everyone shares the desired outcome of benefiting from a common interest.

It does take everyone working together to achieve a common goal. Yet I also recognize that we are individuals. As a result, the Everybody Paddles concept would seem to contradict the American mantra of self-dependence and individualism. It doesn't. Let me explain why.

Great thinkers have often stressed individuality. I love a famous quotation from Hillel—one of the greatest sages in Jewish history—that encapsulates so much of what I want to say in this book:

"If I am not for myself, who will be? If I am only for myself, what am I? If not now, when?"[1]

With this perfect wording, uttered in first-century Jerusalem, Hillel was saying what I had been thinking all the while as the CEO of a social service agency: Stand up for yourself. Take responsibility and act as if you are alone during the crucial fights and moments. But also always remember that human beings need one another, and "the other person is you." When individuals with integrity join together with others of equal stature, they can paddle forward in confidence, trusting one another, to achieve what they set out to accomplish.

Hillel introduced the concept of individuality, getting people to think about who they were. But according to historian Jacob Burchardt, it wasn't until the Late Middle Ages—toward the beginning of the Renaissance, the time of rebirth of Western culture—that the concept truly began to catch on.

> During the Middle Ages the veil covering human souls was a cloth of faith, biases, ignorance and illusions . . . in so far as the human being was considered only as belonging to a race, a population, a party, a corporation, a family or any other forms of "community." For the first time, it was Italy that [broke] this veil and dictated the "objective" study of the State and other worldly things. This new way of considering reality aside, it further developed the "subjective" aspect, and man becomes "individual," spiritual, assuming his new status' consciousness.[2]

America was founded soon after the end of the Renaissance in Europe by bold individuals who dared to sail thousands of miles across dangerous seas to an unknown land. As a result, Americans have always prided themselves on rugged individuality and acclaimed anyone with that perceived personality: mountain men and heroic soldiers Daniel Boone, Kit Carson, and Sergeant Alvin York come to mind.

The concept is stressed in our times. Donald Trump, a somewhat controversial businessman and developer who has helped many people lead productive lives, said about leadership, "You are a one-man army."[3] I agree. Yes, you are when you need to be.

The promotion of individuality, however, is only a façade. The web that unites us becomes clearly visible during tragedies, such as the terrorist attacks on September 11, 2001, or the Boston Marathon bombings on April 15, 2013. In both cases, communities around the country banded together to show their solidarity with the victims in each great city.

The same thing happened during the Iranian hostage crisis in the late 1970s, when yellow ribbons served as the symbol of American unity. Our individual opinions and political differences were smoothed over by the desire to present a united front as Americans.

Americans may talk about "I" but are acutely aware that the better pronoun is "We." We often work as individuals in a group setting. That approach provides opportunities for creativity while helping the organization reach toward its goal.

To promote this reality, I outline strategies that have been proven to modify attitudes, capabilities, and efforts, acknowledging that everybody within a given company must actively participate in the advancement of that company's mission, vision, value structure, and deliverables.

To add practical experience to each principled approach, I have asked thought leaders and influencers to contribute their accounts of building consensus. These unique perspectives on the principles outlined in the book appear at the end of each chapter.

By the time you have finished reading this book, you will have a blueprint for building and maintaining company consensus. You will know how to make sure that everyone on your team is inside the boat, paddling with singular focus toward the desired destination.

Principle One

UNITY STABILIZES THE BOAT

Focusing on individuals who are building teams inside an organization raises two important questions: (1) What separates us? and (2) What brings us together? (The goal of the second question is so we can work hard and achieve great things.)

Every organization—whether a group, a company, an association, or any other entity that relies on the cooperation between its members—is simply a collection of individuals. As a result, the success of any organization depends totally on individuals. Obviously, most of us want to achieve success both on an individual and on a group level. We identify with success: Winning sports teams gain followers, for example. WE win, not just the team.

An excellent organization has quality people who have been allowed over the course of their lives to develop great qualities like independence (responsibility), creativity (permissive flexibility), and accountability (getting the job done), but who can also cooperate and subordinate themselves when necessary to the mission at hand inside the organization. So, the core requirement of team building is a certain amount of freedom that both develops an individual and creates collective discipline. Unfortunately, not every organization can do that. And this brings us back to the first of our two fundamental questions.

What Separates Us?

There's no question that we have a hard time working together, whether in our families or on the job. According to the most recent U.S. Census Bureau report, the divorce rate of first-time marriages is 41 percent; second marriages, 60 percent; and third marriages, 73 percent. That's a lot of dissension.

Some of that comes from our upbringing. For most of us, the pronouns we were most familiar with were *I* and *me*. Conversations typically emphasized how much *I* wanted to accomplish my career goals, how stressful the whole process was for *me*, how I could better a better *me*, and so on. Country singer Roy Clark encapsulated this notion of total self-absorption in his popular 1969 song "Yesterday, When I Was Young."[1]

Early in my career, the more I focused on where I wanted to go, the less I focused on ways to achieve the success I craved.

As I matured, however, I began to realize that *we* meant much more than *I*.

Another element that often keeps us apart involves how we perceive one another. Humans developed as members of small clans, and anyone not within that family unit was considered an enemy. We now have developed far more sophisticated relationships, but our brains still contain the primitive elements inherited from our hunter-gatherer forebears.

Us vs. We or They

As a result of how we perceive one another, we inherently assign everyone to a category, either We or They. "They" are everyone else who looks or acts a little differently. So, for centuries, groups of people have been discriminated against by other groups because of their gender, ethnicity, religion, age, or socioeconomic class. This blind prejudice has led to inequality, mass murder, and enslavement.

Our country is no exception. Throughout U.S. history, we have witnessed great periods when every American has been asked to align him- or herself with American values. These usually occurred during times of war or injustice: For example, during World War I and World War II, women were asked to support men particularly by working in various industries; during the civil rights movement, to secure equality for African Americans, women rallied for constant unity at home, at work, and in the voting booth; and, most recently, after 9/11, Americans united against world terrorists. That's why President George W. Bush's ringing declaration that you are "for us or against us" struck such a chord with so many people. That same attitude spiced up the Vietnam War era, when bumper stickers proudly proclaimed "America: Love It or Leave It."

In the United States, the divisions have often focused on gender, sexual identity, and race. Discrimination has often resulted. Individuals are defined as *they* are stereotyped and isolated from the rest of the society, which believes *they* are nothing more than the embodiment of the perceived notions of those who consider themselves a superior *we*. Within our society, discrimination is rampant and on most occasions crippling, effectively demoralizing people without reason.

I know about this firsthand. I was an individual inside a family, and I was also part of a larger group of the local community. We lived inside the dangerous Brooklyn projects, but it was clear to outsiders that as a family we were different. We stood out by certain peculiarities in our behavior.

What probably set us apart most from American Blacks inside the projects was our West Indian blood. My mother is a Black woman from the southern United States; my father is a Black man from Barbados. We walked in and out of the buildings in single file, like a small military regiment, played together, and kept to ourselves. My parents and grandparents were strict, and I learned to be the same with my brothers and sisters: I was usually telling them what to do. We participated in our own Caribbean culture-based church groups that were very tight communities. As a result, the neighbors usually left us alone.

My separation continued as a Black man in the legal profession and as a CEO among my middle managers and coworkers. I learned that how I handle the perceived differences is critical to my own well-being and success.

I also found that there is a fine line between being different and alienating the larger group around me. Every social organization around me tends to be tribal in some way, and I stand out in any number of ways, including by being different culturally or professionally or because of my social status or religious affiliation. And there are subtribes within the tribes. The way I talk or dress is often enough to stir animosity or suspicion if I inadvertently cross the line into another group.

Those distinctions begin to fade, however, once we realize that we really aren't different: We are all trying to survive every day. After all, today through genetic research we know there's no such thing as race. In fact, there's no *we* or *they*; there is only *us*. We are all the same, divided only by our own individual abilities and not by any artificial aspect of appearance, religion, or gender. We are not forced to limit ourselves or anyone else with these manufactured perimeters.

As the Indian philosopher B. R. Ambedkar said, "We have

liberty in order to reform our social system, which is full of inequality, discrimination and other things which conflict with our fundamental rights."[2]

The Generation Gap

A third element that separates us involves generations, each of which is different. Back in Ancient Greece, Plato complained about the younger generation of his day. In truth, though, at that time there wasn't much difference between one set of children and the next. Most of humanity lived similar lives for centuries: Sons followed fathers into professions; women learned to be housewives. But that's not really true anymore, at least on a behavioral level.

That consistency was shattered in the nineteenth century as factories began siphoning children off from farms and creating the urban sprawl of modern society. The differences became even more apparent in the twentieth century. Famed newsman Tom Brokaw wrote about Americans who endured the Depression followed by World War II, calling them the "Greatest Generation" in his popular book of the same name. People who lived through such cataclysmic turning points didn't complain; they survived.

The next generations, however, were catered to and pampered. The excesses of the 1960s, tempered by the Vietnam War, reflected the results of overindulgence. The process has continued, creating what New York City behavioral scientist

Deborah Bright names "entitleists." They shun responsibility for their own behavior. Of course, they happily take credit for any good things that happen. They rarely see how their actions affect others. They don't see themselves as part of a team, but rather as individuals with others around them. They expect promotions and raises based totally on their presence, not their actions.

Their children are even further from what had been the norm. Generation Y, also known as the "Millennials," consists of 80 million young people born between 1980 and 1995. They represent the fastest-growing segment of the American workforce today. In many ways, Gen Y varies greatly from any previous generation. For starters, they were born in a world awash in technology. They don't know anything else and consider their parents woefully ignorant in that area. For them, cell phones, computers, and the Internet are necessities and have always existed. They are always connected via headphones or earplugs, their eyes riveted on some screen.

Divided by Technology?

In a recent AT&T commercial, the camera revealed people everywhere listening to music playing through their phones. They were in crowded libraries, on the subway, at the beach, or walking down the street, completely oblivious to their surroundings. In October 2009, for example, there was a subway shooting in an American city. A madman chose a victim at random on a train. No one noticed the gun, though the shooter went so far as to wipe his nose with it several times as he taunted people verbally. No one looked up from their smartphones or iPads.

At work or at home, day or night, Generation Yers check their Facebook pages and read email on their iPhone, Black-Berry, or other device. There is no difference between work and private lives; they get personal email, instant messages, texts, and tweets in both places. Their parents isolated the public and private parts of their lives, but Gen Y doesn't see any distinctions.

Millennials also expect immediate answers and instant gratification. They know every piece of equipment and eagerly snap up the latest innovation to come onstream. As a result of that need for immediacy, most recent college graduates are unhappy employees. For example, University of New Hampshire management professor Paul Harvey found that members of Gen Y have a "very inflated sense of self" that leads to "unrealistic expectations" and, ultimately, "chronic disappointment."[3] Their only interests, according to a sepa-rate report in the September 2010 *Journal of Management*, are "high salaries" and "lots of leisure time off the job."[4]

I remember interviewing one young person for an entry-level position. He couldn't write; he simply didn't know how to put two words together in any form. I asked him why he didn't learn even the basics during his years in high school and college. His answer was that he expected his secretary would do his writing for him.

"What happens if you don't have a secretary?" I asked. He wasn't sure (but I knew for certain he wasn't going to have a secretary at our agency).

He didn't get the position he applied for, nor was he unusual. Members of Gen Y have been brought up with everyone telling them that they are great and that they can conquer the world. They believe it. They expect to be the boss the second day after joining some organization. They figure they'll magically float to the top of the ladder. Naturally, with such lofty, implausible goals, they are easily prone to disappointment.

The problem may be simple: Maybe they are just misplaced. Many people have taken jobs they just aren't suited for simply because they needed to find work. That doesn't mean they can't be motivated or capable in a job they like and can handle.

A manager's responsibility is to put an employee in a place where he can achieve the best results. That's the mantra of coaches in sports as well. Successful coaches use the strengths of their team to build success. A baseball manager who relies on home runs to win would be hard pressed to rack up victories with a team long on speed and short on power.

I take that same approach with my agency. Some people might not be good social workers; they may not enjoy working with clients or have the patience necessary to aid disabled clients with severe needs. However, they may be superb in arranging for treatment and identifying resources. They can be vital members of a team by contributing where they can help the most and achieve the most satisfaction at the same time.

Employees who like what they are doing are far more content. "If you're engaged, you know what's expected of you at work, you feel connected to people you work with, and you want to be there," wrote Dr. Jim Harter, Gallup's chief scientist of workplace management and well-being. "You feel a part of something significant, so you're more likely to want to be part of a solution, to be part of a bigger tribe. All that has positive performance consequences for teams and organizations."[5]

However, any employer has to recognize that today's employees are not the same as those of previous generations and to be willing to understand the differences. Gen Y members are fully capable of doing anything; they just work differently. They need to set short- and long-term goals. Helping them do that is part of my job. They also have to realize that goals change; they evolve, just as mine did. I set out to be an accountant and shifted to law, only to end up running a social service agency, which, it turns out, requires knowledge of both accounting and law.

Technology advances are also separating us into haves and have-nots. As I mentioned, Gen Y members in general have no problem with technology; they know—and often purchase—all the most recent upgrades. Many others, however—from both the younger and the older generations—are not as comfortable with high-tech devices. They either can't afford the latest innovation or simply lack interest in learning how to use it. These persons are increasingly relegated to lower-paying, less glamorous positions while silently envying the successful characters portrayed on television and in the movies.

No doubt, there are factors in addition to those outlined above that keep us subdivided. It's all too easy to figure out what keeps us apart; the second fundamental question is harder to answer.

What Brings Us Together?

What brings people together so that we can work hard and achieve great things?

Leadership

One clear answer to this critical question is leadership. Unfortunately, there is a lack of skilled leaders in workplaces today. A recent Gallup poll found that 70 percent of 100 million full-time workers in this country hate their jobs and often are "roaming the halls, spreading discontent." Earlier surveys from 2008 and 2010 show that negative attitude virtually has not changed despite the passage of years.

Why? Gallup pinned the blame for the majority of disengaged and uninspired workers on bosses who are simply not doing their jobs well. "The managers from hell are creating active disengagement, costing the United States an estimated $450 billion to $550 billion annually," wrote Jim Clifton, the CEO and chairman of Gallup.[6]

Cheryl Connor added in a *Forbes* column: "These employees need better leaders who know how to inspire and motivate them, give them opportunities for development, and treat them with the respect and dignity they each deserve. A third of a person's life is spent in the workplace, sometimes more. If the environment an employee works in is led by an extraordinary leader who cares about their development, it leaves employees with little room to complain."[7]

Leadership involves more than just giving often-irrational orders, the favorite ploy of the blowhard boss in the comic *Dilbert.* Instead, leadership involves such areas as communication and identifying others who also have leadership abilities.

I learned that lesson after I became a lobbyist for an organization that represents social service agencies. I had been with the Brooklyn district attorney's office for three years when friends and colleagues recommended I take a job as a lobbyist. A longtime lieutenant of the director, a woman named Louise, was retiring after twenty years. When Louise's choice for the job declined the offer, I was next in line.

I quickly learned why no one else would take the position. For starters, the apartment I occupied when I was in Albany to talk to legislators couldn't have been a more depressing place. It was in a decent location, but not well maintained.

Next, when I tried to discuss the matter with Louise (she had taken a similar position at another company, which meant that we were in meetings together and working on similar issues in Albany), I discovered that she was a bully. She came from privilege—with parents who were wealthy, hardworking, yet elitist types—and she felt entitled. Sadly, her idealism was her justification. While putting herself forward as the central voice for those with disabilities, she simultaneously disabled anyone around her who attracted her disapproval.

Like me, she was a lawyer and a zealous advocate for nonprofits serving the disabled community. It must be said that she did get results as a lobbyist for nonprofit organizations, which are not allowed to lobby legislators directly for funds. Out of the office, after work, she was kind and pleasant. But at work she was more inclined to set up a guillotine than to discuss anything. She eliminated teamwork in order to build herself up as a singular hero, a stifling approach that prevented those around her from growing.

I worked on pins and needles all the time. She chipped away at my self-esteem. I was battle hardened from my years in the DA's office, but Louise was too much for me; I was afraid of her.

The three years I worked under her were intense, but I learned a lot—some of it from her negative example—about being a leader and about myself. I realize in retrospect that I could have done several things differently: (1) by showing more confidence in myself; (2) by asking more questions and demanding more support; (3) by taking more initiative; (4) by continuing my education; (5) by writing better reports and becoming a better inside player; and (6) by confronting Louise when I needed to.

Becoming a Better Leader

I try not to make those mistakes in my job now, and I understand my employees better because of my time under such a leader-dictator. In addition, I came up with one important realization: First and foremost, leaders need followers. How can anyone lead in isolation?

Jesus had an impact only because of his followers, who carried his message to the rest of the world. Louise tried to run the organization alone but ended up simply forcing people to leave or curtailing their abilities to succeed. In the end, the organization suffered right along with her opportunities for greater success.

The way a leader approaches her job and the people she leads determines the success of an organization, but it can also predict failure. At the end of the day, the success of an organization is based on the collective achievements of every member, not just the leader. The functions and responsibilities of every person, as well as every person's ability to achieve the goals set forth by the leader, are essential to the organization's success.

This can be accomplished only through effective communication. In order to articulate the mission, purpose, values, and objectives of an organization, a leader needs to be a skilled communicator. Effective communication is the means by which leaders can achieve their objectives, whether in a business, a family, or elsewhere. The leader must constantly be in "messaging mode."

There should never be a moment when the leader has not taken the opportunity to share important information. From meeting with staff to networking in the community to using social media and pursuing speaking engagements, a leader must constantly communicate his goals and expectations while demonstrating collaboration.

Of course, not everything should be public knowledge. Information should be shared on a need-to-know basis, but if those who need to know don't, then the entire structure is threatened by inefficiency and potential mistakes.

As a CEO, I also realize that every organizational system involves cooperative activities. Among these are the following:

⋄ development of staff or a staff member by supervisors and managers;

⋄ a course of action staff must adhere to and duties they must complete; and

◇ an exchange between employees and their supervisors, and between the CEO and the management team.

A process is involved in every aspect of a business. And each of these cooperative activities must be developed, monitored, and maintained through a process; that is, the manner by which the utilities or departments meet the organization's central goal. An organization cannot run efficiently if a proper and comprehensive process is not in place.

Every process in an organization must include these five factors:

1. an objective
2. a function
3. integrity
4. transparency
5. compliance

As leaders, our approach is always to develop policies, procedures, and processes that will bring the desired result. However, this cannot be the only approach. We must consider what we will do when the policies, procedures, and processes are not followed.

For example, some processes might state that signatures are required on purchase orders and requisition forms. Guess what? A form was submitted without the appropriate signature. A new process must be put in place through which both the person who places the order and the finance clerk thoroughly review each submission.

No system is foolproof. Nonetheless, the leader must consider potential lapses in the operating system.

Mistakes happen. However, they can be considered teaching opportunities rather than an opening to execute someone. We all err, but the goal should be to determine where the process failed and then provide a solution.

Finally, every member of a staff must have specific and measurable responsibilities. Success is attained through the leader's conduct. It is the leader's responsibility to (1) make expectations clear; (2) monitor progress or the lack thereof; and (3) effectively respond to obstacles and shortcomings. This will ensure optimal success in an organization's functioning. Responsibility involves choices, motives, attitudes, foresight, education, training, and professionalism. Conversely, responsibility is about accepting the task of leading the collective unit, in whatever form or context. The responsibility has to be that I/we will do what is right and appropriate; I/we will conduct myself/ourselves within ethical and legal standards; and I/we will acknowledge if our behavior does not support those beliefs.

The core values of a leader are based on his or her integrity; namely, that part of an individual that no one knows in detail but that everyone hopes is good, positive, and moral. It's the part of the individual that must be progressive and demonstrate restraint in given situations, moments, and challenges. This core depends on trust. When signs of shortcomings are observed, disbelief becomes the reality. Top leaders attain enduring success and prominence through professional will and personal humility, accepting criticism as an advantage en route to realizing achievement. Leadership is not about control, being correct, or telling others what to do. Leadership is about nurturing those who are willing to follow you as they, themselves, become better leaders.

Developing New Leaders

Leadership involves developing subordinates who are capable of assuming some of the leader's duties as well as securing a successor. It has been said that if you aren't training your successor, you aren't providing effective leadership.

The first step in this process is identifying a potential leader. This person should not be ego driven. She is instead receptive to feedback, expecting comments rather than turning away or simply denying responsibility. Flexibility is also important, since everything changes; a leader must be able to shift too. A good leader wants the best results, no matter who gets the credit. Being able to share guarantees a better cultural fit. Every organization has its own culture. A leader accepts that culture and is willing to adapt to it and, if possible, improve the negative aspects.

One of the three cornerstones of my agency comes to mind in this discussion about cultivating leaders: my assistant executive director of programs. Along with the assistant executive director of administration and the chief financial officer, she is someone I depend on, because I travel a lot and need employees who can take on leadership roles. I delegate. I must have an executive team who can make good decisions without waiting for me to direct them. Some decisions can't wait.

My assistant executive director of programs was not anyone's idea of a leader at first. A southern Black woman, she was shy and rarely spoke. I saw that she was reliable and that her clients loved her. I really thought she could become a leader, although I doubt she expected to be put in that role since, initially, she was perceived as more of a supporting actor.

She resisted the idea at first, so I moved slowly as I groomed her to become a leader. I would encourage her and give her small tasks. For example, she would take my place at a meeting I could have attended, but where I wanted her to have the responsibility of representing our agency. Over time, I gave her more responsibility. I asked for her opinion on major decisions and tried to treat her like a partner.

As the feedback loop expanded, she felt more confident that I was not just listening to her opinion for form's sake, but respecting what she had to say and acting on it. She now holds a prominent and important position. She's responsible and incredibly capable. Today she is a role model to many of the women on our staff. They treat her as the leader—and that's fine with me.

The same process can work with an entire organization or just a couple of people. As Sun Tzu, the noted Chinese general and strategist of the seventh century, wrote in *The Art of War*, "Managing few is the same as managing many." This is an intriguing thought for any leader—profound, really. Imagine a pyramid-like structure of power that just keeps moving up to a single man or woman or a small board of directors with handpicked officers who manage hundreds or even millions of people.

I have learned something else about leadership: knowing when to engage, and when to stand back and say nothing. This is a skill that I developed with seven frenetic brothers and sisters who were all screaming to have their needs met—not at every moment, but certainly at every other moment.

They helped me learn when to fight and when not to. I learned Muhammad Ali's "Rope a Dope" and other defensive techniques. I learned that a strong person is also wise and does not need to use conflict all the time. You observe patterns around you and learn when to disengage from inappropriate behavior. For example, I learned not to waste energy on insignificant situations—to pick my battles.

The new leaders are waiting for us. Many young graduates want to be in charge, make decisions, and lead companies. It's our job to guide them and help them understand that leadership comes with a price.

Noted humanitarian Helen Keller, who overcame profound disabilities, once said, "Life is either a daring adventure or nothing."[8] It takes courage and determination to take the adventure, and even more to see it through. Courageous leaders experience as many obstacles and as much fear as anyone else; they just don't let it paralyze them. They accomplish this by replacing "I can't" with "I will," and this allows them to continue.

Overcoming the Tendency Toward Separation

As freethinking people, we can modify our social systems to incorporate the fundamental and unalienable rights of everyone. We can end discrimination by working as individuals toward a common goal. After all, the efforts to suture the wounds within society—notably the civil rights movement, the feminist movement, and so on—have been led by strong individuals such as Dr. Martin Luther King Jr. and Betty Friedan.

Alongside these leaders, we can work together to dismantle the societal norms that justify discrimination. Eradicating prejudice within our society begins at the most basic levels of beliefs and ideologies. Historically, there has yet to be a society that exists without discrimination or micro-aggression, but that does not mean it cannot be done. As children, we don't automatically know about discrimination and prejudice, being fearful or biased against someone because of their skin color or facial features or culture. Those are learned behaviors, taught and modeled and passed down from older generations to younger ones. Oscar Hammerstein II made this abundantly—and cleverly—clear in his heartrending lyrics for the song "You've Got to Be Carefully Taught" from the Broadway musical *South Pacific*.[9]

Working together, we can do away with the destructive forces of prejudice and discrimination. Instead of grouping individuals into categories, we must appreciate diversity, encourage individuality, and practice unity. We can set the example for our children who, in turn, will produce generations who no longer see people of different backgrounds or life experiences as part of anything else but the human race. At that point, there will be only *us*, each holding a paddle and moving toward a common destination.

Teamwork: Some History

Teamwork has been the norm in industry since the late 1700s. That's when inventor Eli Whitney, better known for his cotton gin, came up with the idea of an assembly line to assemble guns for the U.S. government. Before that, society stressed individual creativity and effort. Sure, artists like Michelangelo had assistants, but he did most of the work and sculpting. You don't think of him—or any other prominent artist, writer, or leader, for that matter—as part of a team.

The Industrial Revolution of the 1800s, with the introduction of steam power and then electric energy, forced everyone to turn to teams. Individuality was replaced by unions and massive factories where teamwork resulted in the production of products. Henry Ford, the auto magnate, helped refine the system by perfecting the assembly line to produce cars cheap enough for the average consumer.

Americans have been on a teamwork kick ever since. Bruce Piasecki, author of *Doing More with Teams: The New Way of Winning*, explained the need for teamwork this way:

> Teams expand the human experience. They extend our wings in practical, pragmatic, and measurable ways. People who would not normally be able to succeed alone—the planners, the doers, those who lack the internal spark to market themselves—can reap the benefits of success in the context of teams . . . Teams are more important in a global economy than they've ever been before. Standing out in a crowded marketplace takes constant innovation and the ability to get fast results. With the complexity of today's workplace, even the most brilliant individual is not likely to have the skill set to take projects from start to finish. The ability to collaborate is everything, and that requires high-functioning teams.[10]

The concept sounds great, but in reality, many people are very selfish. All of us have the tendency to be egotistical, even though many of us may not be willing to admit it. We often just get so caught up with *I* that we don't notice the *we*. The challenge then is to realize that we will go much further if we channel our energies into forward movement rather than attempting to travel the road alone.

Even individuals who seemingly achieved success based on their own efforts, such as inventor Thomas Edison, really didn't. In Edison's case, people sponsored him, encouraged him, and finally helped promote his inventions. The same thing happens with great artists.

I recognize this truth in my own life. I learned all about teamwork as a kid growing up in Brooklyn with seven brothers and sisters. Both of my parents worked away from the house all day, so we had to handle the chores. As the eldest, I got up early to make sure everyone got off to school, and I babysat at the end of the day. All of us had our assigned roles in the family.

My family is very religious. As a result, I also read about teamwork in the Bible. For example, Deborah, a prominent Israelite leader in the Book of Judges, didn't call for just one tribe to fight the Canaanites; she invited all the tribes to work as a team. In the New Testament, I read about how the disciples also worked as a team to spread the Gospel.

I also worked on teams with classmates. My high school

relied on team teaching, which we thought was the way to even up the sides between teachers and students. When I graduated, I became even more aware of the importance of teamwork. I could never have become an attorney without the assistance of family members who encouraged me, teachers who tutored me, and colleagues who helped motivate me. I just didn't notice how many people were involved in my success.

Now, as head of a major social service agency that provides assistance to mentally and physically disabled residents throughout New York City, I am acutely aware of the teamwork that's necessary to get help to the people who need it. Social workers, direct care staff, and administrators have to work in unison to achieve the optimum results.

◆   ◆   ◆

With good leadership, any group of employees can learn to work together. In the related, brief "Perspective" essay that follows, Kennedy Swaratsingh speaks about necessary unity among the Caribbean Islands. "The message of the 'Everybody Paddles' movement resonates with me," he says, "because I would like to impress upon the leaders of this region the need to focus on a common goal and then ask ourselves what we need to do to go in the same direction." Kennedy has a valid point. Whether the "team" is made up of a group of individuals sharing a common mission or a group of islands sharing common economic goals, nothing happens until everybody is in the same boat, paddling in the same direction with coordinated effort. I admire Kennedy's grasp of the challenges and importance of forging teams across national and cultural boundaries.

PERSPECTIVE: UNIFICATION OF THE CARIBBEAN REGION

Kennedy Swaratsingh, Principal Consultant
at Kennedy Consultants

I first met Charles A. Montorio-Archer in Barbados at the launch of an earlier edition of *Everybody Paddles*. I then had the opportunity to chat with him after reading the book, and I realized that the concepts in his book were very close to my own philosophy.

I spent twenty years as a Catholic priest in Trinidad, also serving as a chaplain in the Defense Force. I was also a member of the Parliament of Trinidad and Tobago.

My philosophy has always been that we are not divided by the Caribbean Sea but rather that we are united by it. Because of our size and geographic location, we should be more inclined to work as one family, moving in the same direction. My political and philosophical underpinnings are corroborated by Charles's book.

Here is a dollars-and-cents example: We replicate things in each island that we could build once and use often. Instead, we build it three, four, five, or six times. From an economic perspective, this is rather inefficient.

The formation of the European Union postdated our regional experience of unity. There was an earlier attempt to form a similar federation in the Caribbean that did not get off the ground. We do have CARICOM, a regional group where we try to work and negotiate as a region, but for a number of reasons we continue to be challenged by issues of sovereignty and isolation. So, ironically, an American traveler can come into our islands with only an ID card, but Caribbean citizens still need passports to go from island to island. These examples exhibit symptoms of disunity and dysfunctionality.

In fact, the only two real enduring examples of Caribbean unity are the West Indies cricket team and the University of the West Indies. Otherwise, we compete as individual nations for the same business, sometimes to our own detriment.

When I was younger, I participated in a youth group where we used to sing "United We Stand, Divided We Fall." In the Caribbean, we have not learned this lesson. I feel that the Caribbean will not attain its full potential until we have learned to celebrate our unique differences as something to be encouraged and embraced and not as something to divide us. And we must also learn to take collective advantage of our strengths.

For example, the landmass of Guyana has enough acreage to feed the entire Caribbean, while Trinidad has sufficient energy to help the entire region manage its energy costs, yet we cannot seem to find a way to leverage the best of what each island brings. So, as a regional consultant, I try to find ways to utilize the talent of the region. We need to develop leaders, but more importantly, we need to develop a philosophy that guides what we do. There must be a commitment in the region to moving in the same direction, coming together and coalescing around certain fundamental principles.

What holds us back from doing that? Certainly, sovereignty is a sticky issue. Particularly in difficult economic times, as elected officials revert back to what is good for their own islands, we have become more protectionist. Thus far, elected leaders of the region have lacked either the will or a way to harness the collective talent and energy of the region to move it in a particular and determined direction.

My graduate study has focused on leadership, emphasizing how Caribbean island nations can use the modern tools available to them in order to prosper. We continue to pay more for goods and services than we would if the region were more connected. For that to happen, elected leadership needs to focus on sustainable development. We cannot afford to continue to be left behind by a world that is moving forward at a much greater pace.

The message of the "Everybody Paddles" movement resonates with me because I would like to impress upon the leaders of this region the need to focus on a common goal and then ask ourselves what we need to do to go in the same direction. We have to overcome our "island mentality." The wonderful familiarity of small-island living can be accompanied by a very limiting parochial perspective. As I learned from my service as a chaplain in the Defense Force, talk gets you only so far. It wasn't until I participated in drills as a regular member of the army that I was accepted. One of the things I had to learn was to let others in the group lead me, knowing that we were all in it together, working toward a common goal.

If we could just get the countries of the Caribbean to unite in pursuit of their common interests, one can only imagine the possibilities for what I believe is the greatest region on Earth.

PERSPECTIVE: GO FAR, GO TOGETHER

Andrea Durbin, Chief Executive Officer,
Illinois Collaboration on Youth

In reflecting on the principle that Unity Stabilizes the Boat, I look back at nine years leading a coalition of community-based nonprofit organizations serving children and youth. As the leader of a coalition, it is my responsibility to gain consensus from the members on the course we are charting. Our coalition risks falling apart if we don't have unity about what we are trying to accomplish and a sense of inclusion so that people feel heard and respected.

It can feel frustrating to invest the time and effort to attend to that process of building consensus. Sometimes the outcome seems so clear cut and predictable that spending time to get input and check in with everyone seems like a waste of time, but I learned the hard way that rushing through does not necessarily get you where you want to go.

When I was first hired to lead the Illinois Collaboration on Youth (ICOY) in 2012, we were a small but fast-growing coalition of youth-serving organizations. Our founder and longtime leader was known as a back-room-deal kind of guy. He was a visionary, but impatient with process. He got things done and saw little value in the tedious effort of checking in with people who were not immediately on board with his ideas. "Get on board or get out of the way" seemed to be his approach. It is funny in retrospect that our name had the word collaboration in it, because it seemed like we did little actual collaborating.

There was another association, slightly older than ours and slightly larger, working in a similar space; providers mostly chose to belong to one or the other. People kept pointing out the duplication and lack of coordination between the two coalitions. I think the other association was viewed as the longtime authority that was set in its ways, and we were the disruptive upstart. As the new leader, I was often asked why there were two associations and why didn't we just merge? My initial answer was to shrug and say that it was a decision that the boards of directors of both organizations had to make. In reality, we functioned as rivals, competing for membership and recognition in our state capitol as the primary voice of services to children and youth.

As ICOY continued to grow, there was an effort by a few providers who were members of both associations to try to force the issue. A working group made of board members from each association was appointed, and they started to talk, but they did not appear to agree on much. There were too many hot-button issues to talk through or around, like who would be merging with whom. Who would be the leader of the merged organization? What would it be called? Rumors and resentments over past slights or misunderstandings hummed in the background but were not addressed directly. The other executive director and I were excluded from the conversations. There were some half-hearted attempts to do some joint advocacy together, but those efforts did not achieve anything significant. After several months, the meetings ended up fading away.

But the idea didn't. And over time, more and more providers began asking those same questions and getting used to the idea that one unified association could have a more powerful advocacy voice while eliminating duplication and controlling costs for members. At the same time, state funding for community services was in peril, adding urgency to the need for a stronger advocacy effort.

Eighteen months after the first effort failed, a new joint working group was appointed, and this time the executives were included. This time, the group decided to hire a neutral facilitator to shepherd us through the process. The first joint project we did was to write a request for proposals for a facilitator and to evaluate the ones that came in. We also applied for a grant from a foundation to support the merger effort. Working through that process, which was a step removed from the delicate conversations that abound during a potential merger, allowed the joint working group to get to know each other and to build trust within the group. We found that we could negotiate with each other and agree on the next steps. We figured out what was worth disagreeing about and what was fine to concede. After the facilitator was hired, we went through a highly structured and focused process that allowed us to work through many challenging issues. Each association checked in with their board and membership regularly throughout the negotiations and received approval to keep moving forward. After several months, we arrived at the conclusion that people had been predicting for years—that the two associations should merge and become one.

Today, three and a half years after the merger, we are a strong and thriving coalition. We have grown our membership by 25 percent since the merger took place, adding in new members that were not a part of either of the old associations. I am confident that this would not have occurred if we had not invested the time to listen, to let people's voices be heard, and even for people to grieve the loss of institutions that had been around for their entire professional careers. Openness, transparency, and patience were key to overcoming distrust and building consensus.

We have even invested our own resources as a coalition to be more inclusive. A few years ago, we started to drill down on why our association, like so many, was dominated by White-led organizations. We invested time and effort to ask questions and to listen to the answers we got. We drafted ideas to address the problem and went back to ask again and listen some more. The result has been a pilot of the Equity and Access Fund, where our traditional membership contributes funds to subsidize memberships for organizations that have historically been overlooked by the philanthropic community and without sophisticated development departments. I am proud to say that we met our first-year goals for the program both in terms of funds raised and new members engaged, despite a worldwide pandemic! And I believe that our advocacy voice is stronger and more authentic as a result.

Sometimes I find myself getting impatient or getting pressure from a member or two to move quickly in a certain direction. When that happens, I take a deep breath and remember the old proverb, often considered to be of African origin: "If you want to go fast, go alone. If you want to go far, go together." We have big things we want to tackle, so we must invest the time to make sure that everyone is on board.

PERSPECTIVE: IF YOU CAN'T GET OUT, GET INTO IT

Kathy Markeland, Executive Director,

Wisconsin Association of Family & Children's Agencies

If you ever have the chance for a conversation with Charles A. Montorio-Archer, I recommend that you take it. His enthusiasm and curiosity are infectious and, as displayed in *Everyone Paddles*, he is deeply committed to exploring the qualities of effective leaders. I will also warn you that getting to know Charles may lead to an invitation to make a future contribution to his leadership ponderings. It's worth the risk.

As a relatively new executive director of a statewide association, there are some key elements of Charles's story that immediately resonated with me. I, like Charles, came into a management role following a career in lobbying and public policy. To be clear, public policy advocacy is still a big part of my job, but at the moment I am engaging in some "on-the-job learning" about leading a small team of professionals. After decades of supporting and representing leaders across the public and private sector ranging from elected county supervisors to church officials and now human services executives, I have many mentors and models to draw on. But, of course, becoming a leader of an organization is a process. It does not happen through osmosis.

There is no magic wisdom imparted with the elevation to a position or the assignment of a title. (As someone who is reading a book on leadership, I would expect that you are in full agreement with this observation.)

Like Charles, I learned early on in my career that leadership and positional authority are not the same thing. The most effective leaders that I have known are humble people—people who are clearly grounded in their own strengths and weaknesses, who are not afraid to admit what they don't know and who measure success by the success of those around them. I have always admired leaders who listen intently and clearly value people. As the brilliant Maya Angelou said, "People will forget what you said. People will forget what you did. But people will never forget how you made them feel."

As an emerging leader, I have found the roles of "decision-maker" and "spokesperson" weighing on me to a degree that I had not anticipated. On my good days, I look to Angelou's words as a reminder that the greatest value I have to offer is not speaking the right word or taking the next most strategic step, but instead in forming authentic relationships. And in a time when the struggles have felt relentless, the uncertainty great—I find anchoring myself and those I support in authentic relationship is helping us weather the storm.

In fact, 2020 was more than a storm. It was a tsunami. As we emerge from the ravages and revelations of 2020, there are three leadership principles in *Everyone Paddles* that I find particularly intriguing: courage, unity, and lifelong learning.

I anticipate that in the wake of the 2020 pandemic and America's reawakening to the specter of racial and social injustice, innumerable reflections on leading through crisis will emerge. Twenty-twenty was many things, including an immersive lesson in courageous leadership. From my vantage point where I have the privilege of working with and for leaders of human services agencies, I was daily inspired by leaders making quick decisions and pivots to keep services up and running while simultaneously supporting a frontline workforce. As a sector designed to support people through traumatic life events, our leaders and our workforce were living the trauma while treating the trauma. To be fair, there was no life or sector left untouched by the turmoil of 2020, but our human services organizations had to continue expending emotional energy when their own emotional tanks were low.

Some equate courage with fearlessness, but courageous leaders know that courage is not the absence of fear; it is the ability to act and take risk despite your fears.

For myself, one of the lessons of 2020 is that we can do hard things quickly when we pull together in the face of a crisis—not unlike the whitewater rafters who inspired Charles. Working in the realm of public policy, I am accustomed to a slow, methodical pace of change; a more cynical voice might label this the grinding gears of bureaucracy. But I am not a cynic. In fact, in my experience, policymakers and professionals engaged in public service are committed to the common good and continuous quality improvement, but they are cautious. There is nothing wrong with caution, but we forget that there is an opportunity cost when we fail to act boldly and take risks.

The benefit of a crisis is that it demands we set caution aside and act. It was energizing to see the creativity of so many people released as traditional restrictions of hierarchy and power relations were set aside. It reminded me of that scene from *Apollo 13* when this group of brilliant people is gathered around a table and someone dumps a bag of random items in front of them and tells them there is limited time, and this is the stuff you have to work with. Work together and solve it. (And, spoiler alert, they did.)

A concrete example of this rapid adaptation was the shift to remote delivery of health and human services via telehealth. We have had the tools and capacity for remote service delivery for decades, but we were on a slow, intentional path toward embracing the technology. We viewed it as somehow substandard to in-person services. As a sector, we were more focused on the barriers than the benefits. One of the most moving stories that I heard about the gift of remote connection was from the realm of foster care. One of my colleagues shared a story with me about a child in a foster home who visited with her mother once a week. As the world shut down, everyone was sheltering in place, which prohibited the weekly connection. The foster parents quickly adapted and found a way each evening for the child to see her mother over Zoom where they read a nighttime story together. This more regular remote connection became even more meaningful in the family's work toward reunification than the prior weekly in-person visits. By integrating the daily connection into the child's life, the visits became a part of the child's routine instead of a weekly break in routine that generated understandable distress and dysregulation. This adaptation in the support options offered to families will continue well past the pandemic when we can once again resume in-person contact. We learned that technology does not replace live connection, but it can greatly enhance connections, and healing can advance more quickly by embracing both.

A unified sense of purpose is a powerful thing. It is one of the elements of running an association that I most value. I have the privilege of pulling people together under a shared sense of mission where the whole becomes greater than the sum of its parts. It was awe-inspiring to see leaders, who are sometimes competitors in the human services world, come together and freely share lessons, resources, and vulnerability with one another.

One of my curiosity questions is how we can sustain that collaboration and forward movement as the crisis abates. We have all experienced that feeling of release after a crisis—that shift into recovery mode that is both necessary and, if left to its own devices, can allow our boat to aimlessly drift. One of the reasons that I am grateful for this invitation from Charles to reflect on leadership at this moment is that it provides the opportunity for focused reflection at just the right time. As I noted, one of the qualities I most admire in leaders is the humility to know what they don't know. Key to sustaining that humility is making space for self-reflection and embracing a spirit of continuous learning.

I was raised by two amazing leaders and lifelong learners who are intentional about both their inner journey and their responsibility to service within their community. While they go about their continuous learning differently, they both modeled the importance of study and reflection. My parents are regularly passing along books and resources and introduced me to one of my favorite books by one of my favorite authors on the topic of leadership, Parker Palmer.

For those who are unfamiliar with Parker Palmer, Wikipedia describes him as an "author . . . who focuses on issues in education, community, leadership, spirituality and social change." As a person raised in a faith tradition, it is Palmer's focus on integrating spirituality with leadership that is particularly compelling for me. In his book *Let Your Life Speak*, he shares how the inner journey is critical to leadership. He says, "[C] onsciousness, yours and mine, can form, deform or reform our world." At the core of Palmer's reflections in *Let Your Life Speak* is his realization that we are all engaged in leadership and followership, and we can engage in these roles consciously or unconsciously. Even if we resist the title of "leader," we lead through our actions and how we carry ourselves in our circles of influence.

So perhaps my meandering thoughts on leadership have taken us full circle. As I stated at the beginning, I would not presume that I have any new or revolutionary observations to share on the topic of leadership, but through the process of reflection, I've come to understand that saying something new is not the point. The point is the reflection itself. Effective leadership begins with self-knowledge and consciousness. From this frame, we are all learners and we are all leaders. There is no getting out of it, so get into it.

PERSPECTIVE: GRACE AND SPACE

Kellie O'Connell, CEO, Lakeview Pantry

The great pivot began the week of March 9, 2020, and like so many in the social impact sector, the team at Lakeview Pantry in Chicago found ourselves needing to quickly pivot our services from inside our well-designed and dignified grocery store–like food pantry space to outside on the street and from cozy, calming therapy rooms to cold, virtual Zoom rooms. The health guidance and protocols changed just as quickly as businesses shut down and the urgent need for free food increased. Even just a year later it is hard to remember how quickly our world was upended.

Cloaked in fear and a deep sense of urgency, my team worked hard to pivot every aspect of our work so we could remain open. At the end of that first week, on March 14, 2020, I sent an email to the Lakeview Pantry team, which read in part:

LVP Fam, these are unprecedented times and I know it's been a worrisome week. Please take care of yourself. Please be patient with me, your manager, volunteers, clients, and with each other. Everyone is scared and anxious about what this all means for us, our community, our country, and our world. In true LVP spirit, give lots of grace and lots of space to those you encounter. Take a deep breath, take a break, wash your hands, read a book, listen to music, exercise, pray/meditate/set your intentions, cook, wash your hands, eat well, hug your loved ones, call or FaceTime a family member or friend and don't talk about the virus, tune out the news for a moment, and get lots of sleep.

In my own personal life and career when I run up against challenging times, I try to eliminate the noise and focus on the next right thing I know to do. Right now, the next right thing is to protect our staff, volunteers, and clients as much as we can and get food to hungry people for as long as we can.

Remember: Grace and Space

Grace and Space became a bit of a personal and internal organizational mantra during the crisis response.

We all needed a little extra grace with ourselves and each other during the very stressful and scary days of the COVID-19 pandemic. With Grace and Space as our mantra, we also held close six key guiding principles we used to make any decisions:

Lakeview Pantry's Guiding Principles during the COVID-19 Hunger Relief Response

- Keep our staff and volunteers safe and healthy.

- Don't make our clients sick.

- Continue to feed hungry people.

- Continue to provide social services (via tele options as needed).

- Continue to support in-kind food donors and service their pickup needs.

- Stay grounded in facts from trusted health experts.

The first week after the great pivot, we all knew there was no feasible way to keep up with the increasing demand and meet the new social distancing health guidance in our existing spaces. Once roomy enough to absorb gradual growth, our spaces were suddenly no longer large enough to accommodate staff and volunteers spread six feet apart, which left us scrambling and determined to get food to our neighbors in need, many of them turning to us for the first time. We started searching for a temporary space to allow us to meet the rising demand and keep staff and volunteers safe. After looking at several suddenly vacant spaces like schools, large event spaces, restaurants, and sports facilities, we found a perfect match: Wrigley Field, home of the Chicago Cubs. Wrigley Field accommodated not only the space required for increased in-kind donations, but also for our volunteers and staff to safely social distance while sorting and packing food to meet the 400% increase in people seeking food assistance during the early months of the pandemic.

With the need and associated fear rising quickly, the iconic Wrigley Field was converted to a food pantry in a matter of days. The ballpark turned out to be a perfect location and offered a long, open air but protected from the elements concourse to create a box-packing line with yards and yards of rollers; freezer and coolers typically used for concessions worked well for frozen protein and perishable dairy; a retail store served as volunteer check-in; and the visitors' bullpen stored the back stock of dry goods in a secure location. Wrigley Field's Wintrust Gate, at the corner of Addison and Sheffield, even turned out to be an ideal location for a drive-thru and walk-up food distribution operation, and the Chicago

Cubs operations staff were critical partners in helping figure out safe and efficient logistics.

The critical and innovative partnership at Wrigley Field lasted for about three months in April–June 2020 and helped Lakeview Pantry serve over 195,000 people during the first year of the pandemic. Challenges related to COVID-19 impacted Chicagoans in a variety of ways, and we saw that directly through a sustained increase in demand for food and mental health support. While we call the Lakeview neighborhood of Chicago home, the pantry's work takes us to every corner of the city, and we remain forever grateful to our neighbors, the Chicago Cubs, for stepping up to support those who needed it most during this very difficult year.

My spirit was lifted up by the real heroes in his work—the dedicated staff, army of volunteers, committed partners, and generous community stepping up with lots of grace to help make sure everyone had the food and support they needed to stay nourished and healthy during the pandemic.

PERSPECTIVE: UNITY, EVEN IN THE MIDST OF A HURRICANE

Andry Sweet, President and CEO,
Children's Home Society of Florida

Living in Florida, I am used to storms, both natural and man-made, but nothing could prepare me for the week of October 7, 2018. At the time, I was the COO for a large child welfare organization, Children's Home Society of Florida (CHS). CHS serves children and families from Pensacola to Miami. Whenever there is a hurricane warning, no matter where you are in the state, you prepare . . . everybody gets their paddles ready.

I was supposed to go to Ft. Lauderdale that week, but Hurricane Michael quickly changed those plans for me. Looking back, I can't recall the meeting specifically, but it was important enough for me to drive six hours round trip for a problem that frankly became meaningless within a twenty-four-hour period. Nothing puts a problem in perspective like a hurricane barreling down on your state.

The storm was heading to the Gulf Coast. Our managers from Pensacola to Jacksonville were joking about who would see Jim Cantore first—hospital humor. The reality was that the storm was not threatening to be the biggest storm on record; in fact, it was projected to be a Category 2 or 3 less than forty-eight hours before impact.

We knew the drill. Caseworkers downloaded their case lists, in the event computer systems were down. They put trash bags over the computers to prevent water damage and boarded up the office. They called all their foster families to make sure we knew their evacuation plans. We double and triple-checked our calling tree (from COO, to executive directors, to program directors, to supervisors, to the field caseworkers, clinicians, and home visitors). All were expected to check in as soon as possible after the storm. The truth is everyone was paddling in the same direction; the teams were aligned and ready.

But we weren't ready for Hurricane Michael.

The majority of our sixty-two employees in Panama City, Florida, went to sleep that night in their own homes expecting the storm to land as a Category 2. But by midnight, the winds had intensified to over 160 mph. Houses were destroyed. Many of our team members had to flee in the middle of the night carrying nothing but their children in pajamas and their pets.

By seven a.m., our first post-storm call revealed that none of our employees were accounted for, and all of our attention turned to two priorities: (1) locate our team and (2) ensure the safety of the 540 children on our caseloads. Nothing mattered but those two goals. Every day for six straight weeks, we had calls twice daily: updating our counts, identifying barriers, and breaking them down. In the days following the storm, Maslow's hierarchy of needs became evident.

Within forty-eight hours, we had located all sixty-two team members. More than 60 percent were left homeless. Because so many shelters were damaged, few places were habitable. If our staff had to leave the area, we would certainly lose our workforce—and we would not be able to ensure the safety of the children under our supervision. We had to care for our team first, and they needed housing.

Ironically, beachside just southwest of the storm's eye fared better than inland Panama City. Our executive director from Pensacola and a board member (a real estate broker) knew an owner of beachside condos whose property was not damaged. A few phone calls later, we secured housing for the twenty-four team members and their families who needed shelter, at a significantly discounted price. We had no idea how we were going to pay for this, but we knew without a doubt that they needed a roof over their heads.

Yet even before the immediacy of housing was granted, true to their profession, our frontline team's first priority was helping others. There were children on their caseloads that they feared were at risk, and they wanted to find them immediately.

In a storm's aftermath, people need help, and everyone wants to help . . . and they can, if you steer them. Board members, volunteers, vendors, and coworkers from around the state wanted to help Panama City. So we gave them "**a paddle and a purpose.**"

Paddle One: Our teams needed phones with service that worked, so a communications wizard in Orlando investigated which carriers still had service and secured enough phones for the team . . . but then we had to get the phones to them.

Paddle Two: With cars damaged in the storm, caseworkers needed vehicles. We had to increase our rental fleet, but Panama City didn't have a single vehicle left, so coworkers in Tallahassee picked up vehicles and drove them to Panama City.

Within seventy-two hours, our workers were driving around Panama City (in teams, as there was an elevated safety risk), trying to locate children on their caseloads. Another nonprofit from Pensacola jumped in and offered help to attempt to make visits. We were making progress, but our teams needed even more help. Our Panama City office was completely destroyed. We needed to get into the state's child welfare information system to try and locate relatives because our team didn't have information in the records they retrieved before the storm.

Paddle Three: We empowered our child welfare data teams across the state to start making contacts through text, calls, and social media. Within a week, we reached out to 100 percent of the families we served to confirm their safety and assess their needs. Even days after the storm, our workforce and our clients still needed the basic necessities of food and water.

Paddle Four: We had a beat-up RV sitting in Tampa that was big enough to carry dry goods, water, computers, and phones. We had volunteers drive from city to city, from Tampa to Panama City, stopping at every CHS office on the way to add supplies to the RV and to swap drivers. When the RV arrived in Panama City, it became the hub for the workers to have a small office space from which to access computers and pick up their phones. We didn't realize until it arrived that the RV had its name already painted on the side: "Hurricane."

Paddle Five: Coworkers from around the state donated annual leave time to their peers. We gave the Panama City team time off to meet with FEMA workers to work on their applications for assistance. We went out of our way to listen, to hear what was needed by the team, and to support them.

Not every storm is a Category 5 hurricane, thankfully. But in nonprofit human services work, storms are not uncommon. Our experience from Michael informed our organization about the culture we want. **The care and feeding of team members is essential to the care and feeding of the most vulnerable citizens in our communities.** *Take care of the people taking care of the people, and they won't let you down.* We have "leaned in" to being a trauma-informed organization, supporting the self-care of every single team member.

Our response to Michael did not come without a cost. All in all, the price tag of the storm: the housing and the supplies outside the normal cost of operations exceeded $500,000. We actively sought relief from FEMA, donors, and funders, but in the end, only a portion of the costs were recovered. "Would we do it again?" we asked ourselves. An emphatic, "Yes," but we needed to be capable to respond that way every time. As a result of Hurricane Michael, we started budgeting annual emergency reserves to prepare for the next hurricane (*or even a pandemic*).

Not every nonprofit can afford to do that, but the cost of not doing it can also dismantle a nonprofit, or any other business for that matter. Our willingness to stand by our team and take care of them sent a message to the entire workforce at CHS that they come first . . . "frontline first."

If we hadn't responded the way we did, what would the impact have been . . . to culture, to morale, to turnover?

"Everybody Paddles" teaches us that there is more that unites us than separates us. The hurricane named Michael brought our organization together as "one CHS."

Principle Two

PURPOSE PROVIDES PROPULSION

Although EDCSPIN is a successful social service agency today, it didn't start that way. The agency began as an idea. Growing up, I had seen a lot of people who needed help. Some disabled individuals lived in my apartment building, some in the neighborhood, and some attended my school. I saw how they struggled to obtain daily necessities. Their burdens did not decrease over time, adding pressure to both the disabled persons and their families. Today, an estimated 18 percent of the population has to cope with one or more disabilities. I always wanted to help but was in no position to do so.

During a family trip in 1995, I read about social service agencies in a magazine and decided to see if I could start one. I didn't want to run it; I wanted to create an agency that could continue to provide assistance even if I were no longer actively involved. At that time, my vision was limited to a simple idea:

Find disabled people in need and help them. On the surface, that seemed sufficient—a decade ago. However, the more I became involved in the day-to-day running of the agency, the more I realized that we needed much more: We needed a mission statement and a vision statement.

Definitive Mission

It's important to understand that a mission statement and a vision statement are not the same thing. A mission statement defines the organization's purpose and primary objective and is written for employees and our core audiences. A vision statement also provides a definition of purpose, but with an emphasis on the values of an organization.

I thought these documents would be easy to write—especially the mission statement. After all, I had established my own mission statement years ago: to become a lawyer. I stuck to the goal even though I had to take other jobs en route. I was very persistent.

As I looked at the agency, I certainly could see we needed a mission statement. Employees were eating in the back room, ignoring clients, and making a mess. They punched in and out without any set schedule. No one knew where anyone was.

But knowing we needed a mission statement was no help in actually preparing one. After all, I was a lawyer who had become a manager; I didn't learn from a textbook, but inch by inch through practical experience. I was confident, inspired by Dr. Martin Luther King Jr.'s comment "Faith is taking the first step even when you don't see the whole staircase."[1] I certainly had faith in my abilities, though, and so I began by using the same skills I had learned in the district attorney's office.

I began by reading a variety of mission statements by major corporations.

Having gathered that information, I researched the various definitions of a mission statement. In particular, I liked the one given in *Entrepreneur* magazine: It "captures, in a few succinct sentences, the essence of your business's goals and the philosophies underlying them. Equally important, the mission statement signals what your business is all about to your customers, employees, suppliers and the community."[2] That made sense. But what was our "business all about" at EDCSPIN?

We still wanted to help people, of course. But that didn't give a true picture of the agency's efforts. I ended up writing a series of questions that had to be answered by the mission statement. They included:

- ◇ Why were we in business?
- ◇ Who were our customers?
- ◇ How did we want customers to see us?
- ◇ What did we actually do?
- ◇ How were we different from other agencies?
- ◇ What were our values?

With that questionnaire to work with, the executive team and I began to thrash out the wording. We ended up with a long—but compelling—mission statement that encapsulates our agency:

Evelyn Douglin Center for Serving People in Need's mission is to enhance the quality of life for persons with disabilities and their families.

We BELIEVE that all members of society, with or without disabilities, are entitled to respect and equal opportunities.

We EMPOWER our consumers to strive toward their highest potential, and prepare them to deal effectively with the challenges they may face.

We PROVIDE every service in a spirit of excellence and genuine caring.

We PLEDGE to develop programs and provide services to hard-to-serve individuals, in un-served and underserved communities.

We AIM to be a leader in providing quality, comprehensive services.

We STRIVE to build a better future for the people we serve, today!

We posted our mission statement in our office for employees to see every day and on our website. This mission statement gives our staff a guideline for how to conduct themselves in the office and with clients, a standard that we all strive to meet.

Completing the mission statement represented the first half of my plans. The second half involved the vision statement, which carries more weight than the mission statement since it goes beyond the agency's boundaries.

Vision = Action Plan

Just as with writing our agency's mission statement, I had never worked on a vision statement before, even though I had a personal one. Like most people, I had thought about my future. As I mentioned earlier, I was originally going to be an accountant. I don't know where that career plan came from; perhaps a high school teacher suggested it. Regardless, that was my vision. It changed while I was in college, however, when I realized I could do more by becoming an attorney. I began to focus my energy in that direction and eventually achieved the goal.

Life is funny that way. After getting my law degree, I pictured myself in a glamorous position in the entertainment industry or corporate law. Instead, I'm working with the disabled, learning compassion and humility along the way. Instead of visiting posh mansions, I'm spending my days in the poorer parts of our community. I could never have foreseen that. The Mexicans have a saying: "If you want to make God laugh, tell Him your plans!"

My initial efforts at the agency were concentrated on stabilizing it, rebuilding trust, and reaching out to the community. I was too busy multitasking and managing to think about the agency's vision. And even without a clear vision statement, my—our—efforts were effective. We gradually became more successful and socially important. We began to provide services to clients considered some of the hardest to help: sex offenders, criminals, and the like.

However, as our agency expanded, I realized that we needed a real vision to carry us into the future. Once more I sat down and wrote a list of questions that a vision statement would have to answer.

◇ What does *successful* mean?
◇ How do we measure that?
◇ How do we know when we've achieved it?
◇ What does *socially important* mean?

Communication, discipline, setting standards, and the like are all vital to the survival of an organization. However, as I asked these questions, I soon realized that a vision is even more significant; it is really the most important element in the success of an agency. Vision provides the framework for everything our agency does. The most successful companies in the world have clear visions that allow them to function smoothly.

Creating a vision statement may be the most important function of a leader. A vision holds everyone together, offering a kind of picture of what success looks like. It helps answer the questions that every employee asks about the company, including its goals, position in society, and value. It is coherent: a set formula that won't mutate under pressure or the passage of time.

A good vision inspires people. It helps winnow out ideas that don't fit, since the only opportunities we consider are those that help us achieve our vision, while others can be discarded. Vision provides no blueprint to the future, but it does explain the destination: Where are we going, and how will we get there?

In studying the vision statements of other companies and organizations, I realized that a vision really has two parts: an ideology and an envisioned future. The *Harvard Business Review* called them the yin and yang.

The yin in this approach represents what we stand for and why we exist. It is unchanged: the Ten Commandments of any organization. The yang is the vision of what lies ahead that keeps any organization together regardless of the changes around it. To some, it is the moral philosophy, the "way" that an agency functions.

An organization's yin, or the core values it stands for, helps it endure across decades in an ever-changing society. The authors of the *Harvard Business Review* article "Building Your Company's Vision" noted:

William Procter and James Gamble didn't instill in P&G's culture a focus on product excellence merely as a strategy for success but as an almost religious tenet. And that value has been passed down for more than 15 decades by P&G people. Service to the customer—even to the point of subservience—is a way of life at Nordstrom that traces its roots back to 1901, eight decades before customer service programs became stylish. For Bill Hewlett and David Packard, respect for the individual was first and foremost a deep personal value; they didn't get it from a book or hear it from a management guru. Ralph S. Larsen, CEO of Johnson & Johnson, puts it this way: "The core values embodied in our credo might be a competitive advantage, but that is not why we have them. We have them because they define for us what we stand for, and we would hold them even if they became a competitive disadvantage in certain situations."[3]

On the other hand, the yang, the envisioned future, shows what an organization wants to be, the goal the staff strive for that sometimes requires flexibility in response to outside changes in order to reach it.

As I said, there was no real vision when I arrived at the agency. Everyone worked hard, but without a sense of direction or purpose. I had to spend a lot of time in a lot of meetings with department executives and employees, but we developed a vision that sustains us now.

Breaking It Down: Steps Toward Defining the Vision

The process of creating a vision is not really complicated, but, as with developing a mission statement, it does take time to get the wording right and to focus properly. Above all, the vision must be real and felt by the leadership, not merely a concept that fulfills an image. A core vision is rooted primarily in the best people in an organization, those accountable for building it—mined from the deeply moral aspects of personality, from our deepest principles. Vision is not necessarily something imposed from the outside, from books, or through other people's ideas.

After all, we all have visions and dreams. But men and women working on a corporate vision can get sidetracked into discussions of their future retirement or plans to start a family. In our meetings we had to concentrate totally on the agency's future.

Where did we expect to be in ten years? Twenty? How were we going to get there? That was the vision we had to see and explain.

First, we had to pick a target year because what we could envision for ten years ahead might be totally different for a hundred. We decided to look five years into the future; that seemed like a nice compromise. Five years may seem like a long time, but it really isn't.

Meanwhile, through my research, I found out we were pretty typical. Organizational visions run from two to ten years, with five years being a convenient middle ground.

We started the actual creation process by looking at what we had accomplished. In the ten years the agency had existed, we had helped thousands of people. We had won several community awards and achieved some positive coverage in the media. These were things to be proud of. These awards and the other recognition become the stepping-stones to future success. They provided the positive platform that a vision could be built on.

Once we knew how long a period of time the vision should cover and some of the high points we hoped to expand on, we then wrote the first draft. Some people like to agonize over every word. In reality, the first step has to be a creative process. We simply tried to articulate as quickly as possible what we envisioned.

The process allowed for open brainstorming. No suggestion was ignored. Some of the proposals just didn't seem right; others were perfect—we just knew it. Everyone in the meetings had his or her own personal concept of the agency. By articulating them, we were able to see how different they were.

I opened the first session by telling my team members

that we were going to compose something important. As a result, we had to imagine a grand future, not something small and insignificant. That can seem scary, but a good vision has an element of fear in it; fear drives us to succeed. I think of Dr. King's "I Have a Dream" speech. That's a real and, in some ways, outlandish vision. Yet, slowly, American society is beginning to achieve it. I wanted something that lofty for our agency.

I told them that we were all busy, so we didn't have years to struggle with this. We needed to work fast, to put into words what all of us were thinking. I wanted them to develop the vision in under an hour. More than that, and we would have been bogged down in picayune word choices and petty differences.

To go fast, we had to reach deep within and draw out our hidden thoughts. It didn't matter to me what other people thought as long as they relayed their hopes and aspirations: the ones nestled deep in their hearts. I also needed them to look ahead. They could not be mired in what was happening right then, but at what could happen, what they wanted to happen. They had to pretend that, in fact, the agency had succeeded. What would be the ideal situation? That's what the vision should encapsulate. It also had to be personal: What did you want to see happen with your position? The personal element feeds into the overall agency vision.

Although computers, iPads, and other devices have created a high-tech world, I deliberately used a blackboard for the meeting. I wrote "Draft" as a title and then wrote key words down for everyone to see. My colleagues were not intimi-dated by the throwback method and were very open with their comments and suggestions. I grew to appreciate their understanding of the agency and how they struggled to create a coherent image of it.

Once we had our first version, we put it aside for several days and then met again to reexamine it. Several of us noticed something missing or perhaps a possible word change. I would estimate that most of the original vision survived, but some alterations were made.

Our biggest discussion centered on specificity. A vision statement can be very detailed, after all, or it can be annoy-ingly vague. Visions require clear definitions that allow some kind of measurement. Saying "we will see more clients," for example, is not as motivating as "we will double the number of clients helped in the next five years."

Once the vision statement had gone through a series of drafts, I circulated the final version to people in the agency and presidents of other agencies, regulators, and various opinion leaders outside the agency. They were not as involved with EDCSPIN and thus could offer an unbiased reaction. Employees typically nod their heads and pay little attention; I needed more input than that.

As with our mission statement, we ended up choos-ing a long—but equally compelling—vision statement. The expanded version on our website reads:

EDCSPIN's focus is providing individuals with developmental disabilities and/or mental retardation the opportunity to learn skills needed to reach their highest level of independence, while insuring they experience the same privileges and opportunities enjoyed by all members of our society.

In pursuing the mission of Enhancing the Quality of Life for Persons with Disabilities and Their Families, we pledge to conduct ourselves according to the following values:

PERSONS WITH DISABILITIES FIRST

We will measure everything we do against a simple standard: is this good for the persons with disabilities we serve? If not, we will not do it.

INTEGRITY

We will honor the trust of the families of those we serve and those who pay for our services. We will conduct ourselves ethically and within the law at all times. We will communicate honestly.

RESPECT

We will act with fairness at all times. We appreciate the need to balance work and family life. We respect individual differences. We welcome open communication and promote inclusiveness.

OPPORTUNITY

We value teamwork and the need to have everyone paddling at the same time, in the same direction, toward the same goal. We want our employees to grow so the reach of our good works can also grow.

We seek to recognize effort and achievement and to express gratitude for jobs done well.

ACCOUNTABILITY

We are accountable for the proper use of funds. We are committed to transparent reporting that is so essential to healthy and trusting relationships.

TOGETHERNESS

We value each other and believe no one's role is more important than another's. We are all about serving those in need and we are all in this together, working to enhance the lives of those we serve.

"Make It So": Implementing the Vision

Once we had developed the vision, we began the process of promoting it. We wanted everyone to buy in, to pick up an oar and join the rest of us who were already paddling.

At our next staff meeting, I presented the outline. To many people, a vision statement is just empty words; they have already heard such talk before. I demonstrated its importance in my approach, keeping direct eye contact and expressing myself enthusiastically. That kind of energy can be infectious.

I also had to challenge the staff to read the vision statement and to accept it. They had to know that following the vision required effort. It forced them to change, to match their actions to the vision. They also had to understand what the vision meant. I am direct and use a vocabulary that's appropriate for my employees. Buzzwords have their place, but not in a frank discussion.

In addition, I let the employees know what specific tasks, actions, and behaviors I expected them to do to be sure the vision had meaning. Our vision statement easily translates into day-to-day activities.

Most importantly, I told them how the vision statement served as my guideline. In that way, I modeled use of the vision and demonstrated that it really did have a purpose.

Nevertheless, it took a while to sink in. Staffers had spent years doing what they thought was best. No one was working together in the kind of cohesive action needed for real success. The vision served as a guideline, but only after employees began to see how it allowed them to pull together.

But once the mission and the vision statements were fully integrated into the team culture, everyone finally began to paddle in unison.

◆ ◆ ◆

Theodore Hanley, a doctor from Saint Kitts, writes in his "Perspective" essay about making things happen, being committed to one's work, and helping others. He says, "Medicine is an excellent vehicle for making change and helping other people make changes. I enjoy doing that more than anything else. In my own life, I've made things happen. I enjoy learning." In other words, Dr. Hanley has a firm grasp on his vision—medicine as a vehicle for positive impact—and as you will see, he has pursued that vision relentlessly, drawing others into his mission of healing.

PERSPECTIVE: LEAVE YOUR IMPRINT EVERYWHERE

Theodore Hanley, MD, Medical Director, Waters Anchor Center for Health & Wellness in Saint Kitts and Nevis, West Indies

I was born in 1960 in the countryside in a place called Tabernacle, in a mountainous area on the Caribbean island of Saint Kitts. I was the eldest of five children: three boys and two girls. My mother was the district head nurse and a midwife until we moved to Saint Peters. My parents decided to build a home in Shadwell, which is where I grew up, played cricket and football, debated politics, and dreamed about distant shores.

During my high school years, my mother finally decided that the family needed to leave the Caribbean. Like most Caribbean parents, she wanted to give her five children better access to higher education. After overcoming some ambivalence from my father, the family left Saint Kitts when I was seventeen years old.

I got the idea to become a physician because my mom was in health care. She was a district nurse, which is the equivalent of a nurse practitioner today. I remember meeting the physician she worked with when I was about seven or so. He was very impressive—dashing—and was somebody I wanted to emulate. From then on, I told my mother that I wanted to be a doctor.

When I was in Catholic school, the curriculum was weak on science. I told my parents I wanted to leave private school to attend public school. They were kind of upset and worried that I wanted to go there, but they let me go. In the public school, they were doing chemistry, math, and physics—things I knew I needed to learn to become a doctor.

We arrived in Brooklyn in July 1978, a family of seven with a whole bunch of suitcases. It felt like the hottest day of the year. Before arriving in the United States, I had never lived in an apartment.

I started college my first year in the States. My brothers and sisters did well in high school and would go on to schools like MIT, Cornell, and Wellesley. My parents sacrificed a lot so their children could have the best education, and their example has carried over into my marriage and my family in countless ways.

Before I graduated college, I met Joanne, who became my wife. In a year we had our first child, and then came graduate school, followed by medical school, two more children, and my residency in anesthesia.

It may sound cliché, but you have to really like what you do. I'm not really sure that I always liked what I did during the journey to where I am. But I am quite certain that helping people has been a recurring theme in my life. Medicine is an excellent vehicle for making changes and helping other people make changes. I enjoy doing that more than anything else. In my own life, I've made things happen. I enjoy learning.

I have been in positions of leadership, creating systems and policies to help people become better than what they ever thought they could be. I have had the opportunity to train doctors, lead departments, help people develop into what they want to be, and make changes for the better in health care and other areas of medicine. I was part of a team that transitioned from doing only inpatient surgeries to doing ambulatory surgeries, where people would go in and come out the same day. At the time, that was a cutting-edge development in medicine, and I was the first director of ambulatory surgery at SUNY Downstate Medical Center. I viewed it as a way of increasing access to good medical care for people who need it.

Similarly, in my current position at Woodhull Medical Center, I'm working to improve patients' access to surgery. Our area demographic primarily comprises Black, Hispanic, and Polish populations—all low income. We have some patients who wait more than thirty days to get access to care; I want to improve on that as well as the efficiency of the operating room, safety, patient satisfaction, and the overall volume of surgeries at this institution. These changes have to happen, especially since Brooklyn is ground zero for health care. Our goal is to make sure the hospital looks good and feels good, that our patients are not in pain, that they refer others, and that we provide the best hospital experience our patients have ever had.

I try to pull people along. I want people to do their best all the time. I've also begun to realize that I've learned a lot from my father about being diplomatic. I listen more; I motivate and coach based on my experiences. With every personality, there is a way to motivate and incentivize. As a leader, you have to find out what is important to a person; you have to really get to know what motivates the members of your team. I do whatever I can to make sure that people understand and focus on our common goal of creating the optimum patient experience. Once they understand the goal, I am like a choreographer, organizing very talented resources to work together, at the same time, always with the same goal in mind. When they do, the results can be remarkable.

In addition to my work here, I feel an obligation to improve life in Saint Kitts. Since 2002, I have been more involved with my homeland, going back more frequently. I was involved with a group called Doctors on Call, composed of colleagues from various hospitals in the city. We were invited to bring surgical services to the island. I started a practice there, specializing in pain management.

Collaborating with the Board of Culture, I would also like to bring more literature and arts events to Saint Kitts. Working together with the board, I think I really can make a difference in the quality of people's lives, not just medically, but culturally, also.

PERSPECTIVE: SUCCESSFUL ON PURPOSE

Margarette Purvis, Philanthropic Leader; and
Former President and CEO, Food Bank For New York City

I have been a nonprofit leader for more than twenty-five years. Fifteen of those years were spent in leadership directed at hunger relief. While I was introduced to food banking as Food Bank For New York City's Vice President of Programming and Membership, the perspective I'm sharing is based on my eight-and-a-half years' experience as the organization's president and CEO. I was selected as the CEO in 2011, six years after leaving the organization to lead efforts related to Hurricane Katrina. During the years of my absence, Food Bank merged with Food Change, one of their member agencies, and I formed a consulting firm, creating national programs and establishing and improving charitable brands across the country. Food Bank For New York City is a $100M anti-hunger organization delivering 400,000 meals per day to 1.5 million vulnerable New Yorkers through a network of one thousand member charities.

There are more than two hundred large-scale food banks in America. The work of these organizations is important because of the vital role they play for so many people and communities at their most trying times. They are literal bridges between needs and means. My belief in the organizations' importance is why I will always challenge and encourage thoughtfulness by its leadership and engaged participation by its supporters. Food banks hold the ability to create or negate the importance of health, diversity, and equity for the most vulnerable people in a city and region. They can use their status to act as a depository for any product, or they can use their platform to encourage increased investment and interest where it's needed most. Purpose helps determine and meet the way forward.

Food Bank For New York City was and thankfully continues to be a successful organization with hard-won accomplishments. The dedication of the staff and board is something that should always bring great pride to all lucky enough to be involved in such a worthy mission. I hold a fundamental belief system that all things deemed necessary and successful should happily welcome examination and review of its impact and most specifically its definition of success. Failure to pursue this vital work is tantamount to sabotage and the definition of misguided stewardship. Thankfully I benefitted from the organization's previous board of directors who in 2012 fully endorsed and supported a strategic shift to support the organization's need for increased impact. My journey of leadership with Food Bank was fueled by purpose, and the successes of its impact were not possible without this purpose.

On the surface it would appear that an organization being called a food bank would mean that the organization's purpose would be a clear, agreed-upon nonstarter. Alas, this is not necessarily true. While the name "food bank" is easily tossed between the large-scale citywide charity as well as the neighborhood pantry, they are in fact different types of organizations, holding similar missions but for different audiences at different scales. Every major city has at least one food bank serving the city or region's charity network responsible for the hunger and poverty needs of vulnerable citizens. While more and more food banks have expanded into services for individuals, a food bank's defined role and core responsibility is to serve charities located in communities across that food bank's designated service area.

When I was asked to return to the organization by its board of directors, it followed a merger between the Food Bank and one of its members, a soup kitchen and food pantry in Harlem. The merger was entered into to keep the member charity from closing due to unfortunate fiscal and management challenges. Leadership was aware that charities, like small businesses, close every day. However, in this case, this organization,

Food Change, was known for incubating some innovative antipoverty programs. A merger between the two organizations would allow the city of New York to maintain the most innovative (and well-funded) programs within the charity's portfolio. The merger also offered benefits for Food Bank in the form of an opportunity to receive a more intimate community side footprint.

The merger resulted in a crossroads experienced by many organizations. It highlighted that while a board of directors may approve a future direction, strategic internal leadership is required to make those hoped-for goals a reality. In addition, while mergers are readily encouraged by traditional foundations, rarely is there an acknowledgement of the very real identity crisis that often follows a merger. Mergers sometimes reveal what can be a huge and painful mismatch between a board's vision and the charity's readiness. In fact, my experience taught me that a merger can often be a neat little cover for what may be a messy transition with various alignment land mines discovered over time. The organization I met on my first day as CEO had staff members referring to themselves as "Food Bank vs. Food Change" SEVERAL years after the merger. The staff truly viewed themselves and acted as completely separate entities. The tax program saw zero connection to food, and the meal service program had nothing to do with the schools-based program or SNAP (aka food stamps). The adopted programming of Food Change was operated in isolation from Food Bank programming, meaning NONE of the programs were shared with any of the network of one thousand charity members across the city, regardless of the need or fit. Our listening tour revealed a high internal usage of words like "biggest," "highest," and "greatest." This was excellent intel because it highlighted the organization-wide tendency to measure prowess against self instead of a comparison to impact. I was hired, according to members of the board, to develop and implement a vision and strategy to make sense of and then maximize the decision to merge. In the case of Food Bank For New York City's readiness and propulsion toward a new definition of impact, PURPOSE was more than an oar; it served as structural glue and fuel for the needed paddling.

Even though propulsion, which is defined as the act of driving or pushing forward, often conjures images of big industry or tech, I don't think it could be needed anywhere more than it is at a food bank. Food banks, absent a disaster, are primarily seen, led, and invested in the same way year after year. This is great for stability but likely not as helpful to the number of new families and individuals introduced to hunger every day. Each new hungry individual brings new needs and demands requiring new thinking and engagement. Food banks, while being staples of their communities, can easily fall into a comfortable rhythm, promoting the same programs, same metrics, using the same stories, hoping to maintain the old support and potentially inspire a bit of new. However, when these organizations are led from the needs-based lens of a hungry person and the vulnerable charities trying to serve her, the need for speed, innovation, and the eager pivot are more appreciated. My team's mantra was to "move, think, and LEAD like your loved ones were on those food lines, and never forget their view if they were watching us. Nothing would be more disrespectful than watching comfortable leadership mailing it in just as they did the year before."

To realize the propulsion needed for impact, we had to make some basic yet prominent shifts in how we operated and communicated as an organization. One of our first and most important jobs was to **move the organization toward an identity of one organization with a shared and appreciated understanding of our purpose that we would passionately pursue together.** One of the most important activities we adopted was having the staff write new core values based on the organization's mission. We hoped that their adoption of the new direction would be aided by their engagement in something that would be made front and center to our work. Each core value was assigned a color, and those colors were woven into the brand's art, the colors of the walls, and everything that staff and volunteers would come across along their path each day. It also served to demonstrate to the staff that this way forward was not temporary but the direction for the foreseeable future.

Another key shift was changing our very metric of success. Like all food banks, Food Bank For New York City told its story through a description of pounds of food. The higher the pounds, the more successful the organization appears. Unfortunately, that measure fails to allow a review of food quality, desire, and alignment between distribution and the needs of poor people. We decided, as the recognized leader in the space, to adopt a new measure based on meals, specifically a measure called a meal gap. In essence, we chose to no longer measure ourselves based on the number we were clearly leading in, because it had no real ability to personalize or connect itself to the needs of hungry New Yorkers. Instead, using the lens of purpose, we adopted a measure that highlighted where we (in the form of our programming, food, and leadership) were needed most but were often not found.

We found that like most food banks around the country, 80 percent of our food was going to approximately 20 percent of the charity network. This 20 percent was not found in the poorest communities and did not include the neediest charities. I could quickly see why the meal gap measure was not readily adopted by all. Highlighting the gaps in servicing the needy was uncomfortable and on the surface could have made us lose donors. The new measure required that we think, connect, and critique ourselves and how we made decisions. This led to a review of who was on our team, how often they engaged with our target audience, and where our perspectives found their origin. It didn't just challenge the status quo . . . it highlighted the many ways the status quo was a part of the problem. Purpose-based programming and realigning is scary for many, infuriating for some, but necessary for progress toward meeting the needs of those we were charged to serve.

Another key shift that we made toward purpose involved **examining, changing, and expanding upon the makeup of our leadership team and the partners invited to have a seat at the table.** It was important that we counted more people who did not need hunger, poverty, and community side resource inequity to be explained to those in leadership roles. At my first board meeting, the board of directors in place in 2012 made it clear that while a unified team was paramount, the journey toward identifying and securing that bench was both expected and fully supported. In turn, we actively sought out leaders who understood, shared, and respected the perspective of those seeking and deserving dignity for lives impacted by poverty. I highlight this shift because *the resistance to change the makeup of the voices allowed to lead is often the greatest barrier to purpose and the inherent propulsion and progress it brings.* Only by sitting with more charities in what's referred to as the outer boroughs (Bronx, Queens, Brooklyn, and Staten Island), who were struggling to make great change with little resources, did I learn how often traditional philanthropy groups granted their dollars, desperately needed in the outer boroughs, instead to Manhattan-based charities. These Manhattan groups were deemed more worthy of investment, and then the groups traveled to mentor or even set up shop in needy communities rather than the support going directly to the local, more familiar leaders in the boroughs. Accomplishing our goal to close the meal gap meant that not only could we not replicate common practice, but we had to steadfastly show a commitment to righting the ship and equitably handing out the oars. Failure to do so would make us worse than the status quo and inauthentic in the eyes of the majority of our membership.

My leadership journey was consistently blessed to see a constantly expanded and evolving network of partners and donors who were in lockstep with increased support and passion for the cause and strategic direction. Even with support, our story is no different than any other industry. Change is hard and rarely welcomed even when called out as needed and promised to be supported. Resistance to change is normal and shouldn't be personalized. It should be expected and recognized as conquerable, especially when change is led by purpose. The beauty of adopting a purpose-based lens is that it provides the opportunity to introduce change using language and perspectives already agreed to by most involved in the life of the organization.

In the time that we made purpose a north star, we saw Food Bank grow in stature, and were asked by the governor to chair the state's anti-hunger policies, increasing the number of donors, volunteers, and size of financial gifts while achieving multiple years of clean financial audits and perfect score warehousing reviews. We saw existing corporate, government, and individual donors double and quadruple their existing support as a show of partnership and commitment to our focused intentionality to close the meal gap and narrow in on our purpose. At the time of major hunger policy issues, the organization was often the selected hunger expert on multiple national and international news platforms and speaking circuits. Most importantly, we found that shifting the distribution of food toward the meal gap not only resulted in a higher number of pounds of food distributed but the majority of it going to the poorest communities and people we were responsible to serve. We introduced new metrics, changing produce selections to match the health disparities experienced by poor people in need of green leafy vegetables instead of earning bragging rights based on the weight of heavier items like potatoes. Purpose didn't just help us go forward or faster. It pushed us in the right directions.

Our journey with purpose and propulsion taught me many things. Namely, I learned that:

Purpose is a gift to leadership: It's a difficult request to ask a successful organization to consider change. By utilizing the lens of purpose, it begged leadership from the board to program management to look at poverty and the collective role of leadership's responsibility to impact it in a different way. Purpose-based conversations forced an examination of how our operations impacted the lack of dignity experienced by those we served.

Purpose forces the removal of capes: Heroism is a dirty little secret in the field of human services. It's perfectly understandable. Helping feels good. Being credited with helping can feel even better. Unfortunately, being thought of as a hero can become a bit of a drug, with an addiction that can be hard to break but absolutely necessary to always try. When an organization's purpose is to lessen the perils of poverty and hunger, individual need for attention, credit, and admiration are not only off-putting but dangerous to the bottom line and organization effectiveness. Heroism is a sign of otherness and privilege. It doesn't just suck the air out of a charity's potential; it serves as a constant distraction and aggressive competitor to purpose.

Purpose changes perspective: As a purpose-driven leader of a poverty organization, my job was often about being the key reminder that instead of heroes, we were facilitators of equity, justice, resources, and solutions designated for and desperately needed by vulnerable communities, charities, and people. Purpose was my go-to tool to help ease the treacherous terrain of ego, opportunity, potential product fraud, and change. While it was not always 100 percent effective, it was a necessary and reliable tool in creating impact, trust, and viability. When we started using the lens of purpose, it took us out of a place of doing things the way we always had, or because they were on trend, or because they reflected the desires of a particular donor . . . so we were afraid not to. The lens of purpose created clear boundaries on right and wrong, appropriate and inappropriate, and fit vs. nonfit. Anytime I faced a hunger colleague

who wanted to debate pounds vs. meals, I would immediately think of the pride and evidenced efficiency I
saw in the men and women working in our warehouse.
By simply changing the language concerning their
efforts, reclassifying it to reflect the number of MEALs
they moved to a community, we not only witnessed an
increase in their pride in serving their neighborhoods,
it also led to a 25–30 percent increase in food selection
productivity and reduction in errors and waste.

Paddling is hard, as it should be: Creating positive
change at a food bank sometimes felt like attempting
to parallel park a cruise ship. The hardest part of the
work was honoring and respecting the need to move as
a membership organization with a network exhibiting
great need and desire for help on a backdrop of widely
varying capacities. The tasks making the work hard are
what made it important. Thankfully we understood that
no one floats toward their purpose or true impact. Leaders and teams should expect to extend effort in order to
realize the desired results. It would be great if paddling
alone fueled (and funded) charities. That would mean
that the hardest workers would be guaranteed safety.
Unfortunately, in the world of nonprofit management,
traditional institutional philanthropy is still king, and
funding decisions are often shrouded and protected by
risk-averse decision-making favoring certain profiles,

voices, and the like. As with all things, the best antidote to a limiting status quo is to keep paddling using innovation, organic connection, storytelling, and purpose to create the support and community of committed supporters needed for the awesome and worthwhile journey.

PERSPECTIVE: RAISING PURPOSE

Marlon Rice, Director of Special Projects, Office of the 56th Assembly District and Founder, Good People NYC

As a child, I only had two things that I wanted to do when I grew up. I wanted to write a book, and I wanted to run a marathon.

That's it.

I can remember sitting in my sixth-grade class at Concord Elementary School in Bedford Stuyvesant, Brooklyn. My sixth-grade teacher was Ms. Vicki McMillan, a beautifully brown woman with perfect almond shaped eyes and a voice that was an octave higher than you thought it would be when you first saw her. Our classroom was sunshine yellow, with alphabets and numbers adorning the wall alongside portraits of Shirley Chisholm, Jackie Robinson, and Benjamin Banneker. It was a very intimidating time for me as a student, because I was at least one year and in some cases two years younger than all of my classmates, having skipped the fifth grade during the summer. I can remember feeling like all of my classmates had their entire lives together. They were grown. I was a child, still. This was even more evident when we were tasked with a writing assignment that asked us to explain what we wanted to be when we grew up.

All of my classmates had such precocious answers. Lawyer. Doctor. Police Officer. Each answer explained with such a wonderfully assuring certainty, with every student projecting riches at the end of the yellow brick road. The lawyer was going to be rich. The police officer was going to be rich. The basketball player was going to be rich. Meanwhile, I struggled to explain what I wanted to be when I grew up. Honestly, I didn't want to be anything, and I knew that even as a ten-year-old sixth grader.

I didn't want to be. I wanted to do.

Webster defines purpose as "the reason for which something is done or created, or for which something exists." Purpose is your why. You can ask ten-year-old children across the nation what they want to be when they grow up, and most children are going to answer you in the framework of the same ten to fifteen answers: lawyer, doctor, police officer, athlete. However, very few ten-year-olds will be able to explain to you what they wish to have as their purpose. A conversation about purpose is a layered conversation. It's philosophical and nuanced, and it's simply not the kind of conversation that adults are used to having with children.

However, if you shift the question posed to "What is the reason why?" or "What is your aim or your intention?" that pivot engages a child's mind, compelling them into a discussion on purpose. Ask a child what is the reason why they want to become a doctor, and their answer will expose what that child feels is the purpose behind that career choice.

As far back as I can remember, my parents have communicated with my sisters and me in this way. My father's favorite word was "think." He would always ask our opinions about things. He enjoyed challenging our train of thought. He would ask, "What do you think about so and so?" And if you replied, "I don't know," he would return with, "I didn't ask you what you knew. I asked you what you think." And then he would wait and listen to what we thought, and then he would question that. This line of questioning was more than just a challenge. This was practice. He was teaching us how to process information.

As someone who grew up celebrating Kwanzaa, I've recited the Nguzo Saba hundreds of times. The fifth day of Kwanzaa is Nia, or Purpose. The principle states, "To make our collective vocation the building and developing of our community in order to restore our people to their traditional greatness." Collective vocation is the sum of the things that each of us brings to the table for the whole. You may be great at drawing, and I may be great at math. When we bring those talents together to build and develop our community, we are practicing Nia, or purpose.

The messaging about using your individual talents to build and develop your community was always something that sat well with me. It just made sense. It was the way that I viewed the people in my neighborhood—teachers like Ms. McMillan; Dr. Gardner, who had a private practice on my block; Ms. Taylor, who owned Hillcrest Foods on Nostrand Avenue; Jah Ras, who sold incense near Atlantic Avenue—they were all practicing Nia, bringing their individual talents into the building and development of our community. And for me, they all mattered. Every one of them mattered. The scent of sandalwood that made me smile as I walked past Jah Ras's incense store was as needed to the whole as the sandwich that I purchased from Ms. Taylor's store.

Because of the concept of Nia, I knew early on that my life wouldn't be defined by what I wanted to be. It would be defined by what I wanted to do. My job title wouldn't identify who I am; it would be my actions and the reason behind them that would identify who I am.

I knew this before I knew that I knew it. In the spring of 1986, when I was in Ms. McMillan's class worrying about whether or not my answer on what I wanted to be was good enough, I was actually clarifying my purpose.

Like my father, my mother also played a huge role in shaping my purpose. She is currently legally blind now, but before her degenerative condition took her sight, she was one of the most voracious readers I've ever known. As a child, she would give me these amazing books to read, and demand from me a book report on what I had read. My mother gave me *Roots*. My mother gave me *Flowers in the Attic*. She gave me *Lord of the Flies*, and she gave me *Kindred*. I read them all, and more. It wasn't long before I began falling in love with the differences between the writers I was reading. I loved the bleak, dystopian feeling of *1984*, and I loved the pomp and circumstance high drama of *Julius Caesar*, but most importantly I appreciated the difference in writing styles. The stories were all amazing, but what captured me most were the voices, the way in which the authors spoke to me, a child. I wanted to do that. I wanted a voice. I wanted to say something that would be heard and recognized.

There was something else my mother exposed me to as a child. On the first Sunday of every November, she would take my sisters and me downtown to stand in front of the Brooklyn Academy of Music to watch as the runners of the New York Marathon rolled through. My sisters and I would position ourselves right at the curb so that we could slap hands with the runners passing us. Here we were, in the brisk weather of autumn, with coats and long jeans on, and these runners were in T-shirts and shorts enjoying this seemingly impossible task of running 26.2 miles through the streets of New York City. They would smile at my sisters and me and slap our hands as they passed. We would get especially excited to see a Black runner. We'd scream and try to get their attention as they passed. The marathon seemed impossible, and yet I was there watching every autumn as thousands of runners were proving that it was possible. I wanted to do that. I wanted to challenge myself and to conquer the impossible in the same way that these runners were doing.

Everything that I do in life is rooted in the answer that I gave Ms. McMillan in the spring of '86. I do exactly what I wanted to do when I grew up.

I said that I wanted to write a book, but my purpose in doing so was to curate a voice, to be an agent of communicating what I see in my community, in the nation, and in the world. I learned later that writing is a form of service. I wanted to be of service.

I said that I wanted to run a marathon, but my purpose in doing so was to continually find new challenges to overcome, and to be an example of that strength and resilience to others. I wanted to choose a goal that seemed impossible, and then work to accomplish it. I learned later that doing such a thing requires a significant work ethic. I wanted to build in myself a significant work ethic.

And yes, I've written books and I've run marathons just as I intended. But intention is always the how to the why of purpose. Your intentions will always point in the direction of your purpose.

How do you raise purpose in children?

Neither of my parents were particularly educated people, and to be honest I'm not even sure that either of them had a conscious plan on how to raise purpose in my siblings and me. When I look back on all of it, there was just one constant that I can lift up as an important facet of my upbringing, as it deals with this idea of raising purpose. My parents constantly compelled my sisters and me to process information. In their own way, they have always challenged us to process information. They demanded that we read and gather data, and then they questioned us about that data, over and over again. My mother did it with the book reports. My father did it when he asked me about what we saw on *Tony Brown's Journal*. If you consider that the human brain is like a computer, the ability to process information is so important for its growth and development. The quicker you can process information, the more information you can retain, and the better you become at making decisions reinforced with discernment. A child soaks up data like a sponge. Cognitive processes develop very quickly in the first few years of life. Nourish a child's mind with information and experiences, and that child will grow into a complex thinker, capable of standing firm in their decision-making abilities because as a child you consistently made them defend their decisions.

That's it.

No high science or metaphysical alignment between child and universe is required in order to raise purpose. Simply raise purpose in children by continuously feeding their ability to process information. Feed them data. Challenge their assumptions. Create in them a spirit of discernment. I promise you that your child will take it from there.

PERSPECTIVE: A PURPOSED PERSPECTIVE

Claude A. Robinson, Jr., Executive Vice President of External Affairs & Diversity, UCAN

It was March 10 at approximately 11:24 p.m. CST when I received the call from my oldest son, Dorian, a rising junior away at college in New York City. He stated that the school informed them the campus was closing in three days due to severe concerns regarding coronavirus. He needed to come home immediately. This abrupt life change wasn't in the plans; however, when life changes abruptly, "purpose" is sometimes birthed.

What was planned was a twenty-fifth work anniversary celebration that a coworker had organized. They paid homage to me for over two decades of compassionate service through a phenomenal social service organization, UCAN. Ironically, I received numerous emails and calls from well-wishers saying they couldn't attend due to compromising health conditions. I had listened intently to my son the night before and was now listening intently to others I've known personally and professionally. The ability to listen to one's life purpose is essential to leadership. Additionally, listening to the needs of individuals, teams, and communities is tantamount to effective leadership.

In the most vivid of my dreams, there wasn't a way I could imagine the world would experience political, economic, social, and health-related strife. The pace of life would come to a screeching halt for many but take off at an equilibrium-shaking rate for others. Luckily, or should I say fortunately, purpose always provides propulsion.

UCAN is a 125-year-old organization that strives to build strong youth and families through compassionate healing, education, and empowerment. It is an agency with impactful programs in child welfare, workforce development, education, violence intervention/prevention, youth development, and foster care. In 2020, the pandemic positioned UCAN to exemplify the mission, vision, and values in service to humanity in innovative ways. As author Shawn Achor states: "The most successful people see adversity not as a stumbling block, but as a stepping-stone to greatness." I wholeheartedly believe this statement, as the adversities of 2020 illuminated my inner and outer purpose, propelling me toward immense growth as a leader.

As EVP of External Affairs and Diversity at UCAN, I'm responsible for leading a host of internal/external tasks that interface with essential stakeholders. These tasks involve community relations, government affairs, corporate engagement, spiritual formation, and diversity, equity, and inclusion.

Our community approach's significant pillar was to ENGAGE, EDUCATE, and EMPOWER specific audiences to build friends, neighbors, and ambassadors to enhance our agency brand and reputation. Gaining leadership time and attention across various government, nonprofit, faith, and business sectors presented a significant challenge. Moving past the "vocal opposition," cynicism, and skepticism required a collaborative and egoless approach to relationship management. It was paramount to recognize that there essentially was no proverbial end game but the process of establishing a solid foundation from which to build mutually beneficial relationships with key audiences.

The medical disruption of 2020 provided opportunities to lead through the double pandemics of COVID-19 and civil uprisings caused by the lingering ills of systemic racism and its impact on people of color and an unwitting majority community. For example, UCAN leadership prioritized essential staff through what became known as the "Meal Train," where we ordered, bought, delivered, and served over 1,800 meals at the cost of over $19,000, provided staff a mission commitment bonus, and maintained a consistent, visible presence in our offices and around the community.

Moreover, UCAN leadership pivoted during the pandemics to become a temporary food distribution site in partnership with the Greater Chicago Food Depository and Chicago Beyond to deliver over four tons (7,600 pounds) of food to various grateful organizations, institutions, churches, and individuals. The collaborative partnerships strengthened the original goal of substantive community relations.

"Thank you for your donation of 90 individual boxes [of food]. Currently, we are not funded by the city, state or the federal government and it is individuals like you who help us feed our military veterans. Our staff appreciates your commitment to helping us to help others in need."

—**Daniel Habeel,** President and
Founder, RTW Veteran Center

Addressing the scarcity of personal protective equipment in underserved communities and among many of our program participants was another pur-posed endeavor toward serving the community during chaos and instability. The ability to distribute hand san-itizer and face masks (and encourage the consistent use of both) aided in residents' overall safety.

To propel toward our purpose, leaders must find tangible ways to reflect and renew to realize their vision. In 1967, Dr. Martin Luther King Jr. wrote his final manuscript titled "Where Do We Go from Here: Chaos or Community." Dr. King spoke of better jobs, higher wages, better housing, and education. He focused on the pressing issues that if addressed in the right way, would guarantee the evolution of America into some-thing completely incredible (King, 1967).

It is true that Purpose Provides Propulsion, and it is a vital leadership competence. UCAN established a successful and impactful community relations strategy in this manner. The ultimate goals of being a value-added, community-centered anchor organization were actualized. On March 7, I had the opportunity to make a large food donation to a homeless shelter on the West Side of Chicago. Upon arriving, the faith leader greeted me with the warmest smile and stated how glad he was to see UCAN and that our organization was a true blessing to the community.

Today, despite the life-altering challenges posed by the double pandemics, a deep, abiding feeling is beginning to sweep across the community. A spirit of joy, hope, and optimism abides. It comes from a sense of purpose deep within, the opportunity that arises in the middle of chaos.

PERSPECTIVE: LIVING WITH PURPOSE, PASSION, AND POTENTIAL

Dr. Keith White, Esq., Civil Rights Attorney; Counsel,
Christian Cultural Center and Partner, Bklyn Combine

In the early 1900s, the ice making and distribution business was booming. Ice makers would import, freeze, and warehouse ice to be distributed to neighborhoods throughout the United States. This ice would be cut into big blocks and stored in an icebox that businesses and families would use to store perishable items. This was an essential service for communities in New York City, where there was limited access to affordable refrigeration systems. However in the 1920s, as electricity and affordable refrigerators became more accessible to more communities, the need for iceboxes and ice makers diminished. As refrigerators were purchased by middle and working class families, ice makers went out of business.

While a shift in consumer attitude and opinion may be to blame for why ice makers went out of business, I would submit another reason. Ice makers were not operating in their purpose. It is likely that many ice makers during this period believed that they were in the ice-making business. This fatal flaw was informed by their failure to see the broader purpose for what they provided. Ice makers were not merely in the ice-making business, they were in the refrigeration business. Had ice makers recognized the bigger purpose to their sector of work, they would have pivoted their business development plans and transitioned to refrigeration. A keen understanding of their core purpose would have prevented their extinction and propelled them into profitability.

The first step in analyzing the purpose of anything is considering why it exists. In the example of the ice maker, the ice maker exists to provide refrigeration and preservation to perishable items. However, the ice makers saw their purpose as limited to delivering ice to iceboxes. This gap between their actual purpose and their perceived purpose created a performance deficiency that resulted in their demise. The same can be said for individuals, businesses, and entire sectors of government. If the purpose of a thing is not clearly understood, the potential of that thing cannot be fully realized. However, the more clarity we have in our purpose, the more focused we are in reaching our full potential.

Applying this conceptual framework to nonprofit work is essential to the success of the nonprofit. Organizational purpose should inform the systems and structures that drive a business. I have experience with failing to identify purpose and the decision traps that result in disastrous consequences.

In 2006, I cofounded a nonprofit organization. We formed the entity as a Community Development Corporation with a focus on developing historically marginalized and minoritized communities. Our organization hired consultants and contractors in an effort to procure grants and government development projects.

Although we hired very capable partners, after two years, we failed to procure any government contracts. While we were finalists in several open-bid projects to develop affordable and senior housing, we were unable to close on any projects because we did not have the requisite experience. After several additional attempts at government contracts failed, we closed down the nonprofit.

In retrospect, our failure was not born out of inexperience, it was born out of misunderstanding our purpose. We created a nonprofit to develop the communities that we cared about seeing thrive. However, we focused on obtaining government grants and development projects. The purpose for nonprofit work is to operate in spaces and use nongovernmental methods to improve society where the government is not equipped. But, in relying on government contracts, we committed to a path that was incongruent with our purpose. The space between what we created the organization to do and what we actually focused on created performance gaps and accountability lapses. This was our failure. We did not commit to our purpose and let that propel the work of the organization. Thankfully, this experience can be contrasted with another.

In 2014, I cofounded another nonprofit organization. This organization was also created with a purpose and mission to improve the lives of marginalized and minoritized communities through community development. However, instead of seeking government partnership and projects from the organization's inception, we sought community partners and focused on finding opportunities to build community with local residents. We understood our purpose was tied to our everyday interactions with the community, and we committed to finding every possible way to provide education services, mentoring, and advocacy. After a couple years of doing this work, other organizations and individuals were offering to sponsor our work.

After several successful ventures that resulted in design and development opportunities for our affiliates, government agencies began contacting our organization in an effort to contract with us. This established a principle for us that started as a proof of concept: your purpose will make room for your potential. Or, as Dr. Montorio-Archer has eloquently stated, "Purpose provides propulsion."

THE CAPTAIN SETS THE COURSE, THE WHOLE CREW PADDLES

~

When I look back at all the effort I have expended to make something of my life and at all the complex events and experiences that brought me to where I am, I realize how much of my life has been a balancing act: paying careful attention to my own development and realizing how my needs and wants influence and are influenced by others. We all live alongside other individuals and within groups, and there is an art to navigating our way so that we promote and don't stifle one another.

As I've spoken of in earlier chapters, my family life was the greatest influence on me, as it is for us all.

Then there was college and law school, during which I also helped start EDCSPIN. I left the agency at first to work for the Brooklyn district attorney for three years after completing law school. I then became a lobbyist in Albany for another three years while representing organizations for the disabled, and finally came back in 2007 as CEO of the nonprofit I had helped start, where I still am.

These were all organizations within which I had certain roles and responsibilities. Family is intensely personal, but life at a competitive school like Brooklyn Law or in the workplace at EDCSPIN can quickly become similar to being in a family, taking on elements not only of shared joy or purpose but also of jealousy or rivalry. So, when I look back on it, the dynamic of me versus the group or other individuals was always working, at every stage of my development.

When one reflects on this dynamic, questions invariably arise, including these:

⋄ When should I assert myself, and when should I lay back or compromise?

⋄ Can I actually place certain goals higher than myself? Why would I want to?

⋄ How do I balance empowering others versus self-empowerment?

Taken together, these questions are really asking, how can I be the best leader? That's what I want to focus on in this chapter.

A lot of people who know me tell me I got my earliest training within my family. When I first heard that, I would laugh, but today, I happily acknowledge that it is absolutely the truth. Because of my position in the family, I quickly found myself as the leader.

There was no choice, since I was the eldest and my parents were rarely home because of their jobs. I really didn't know anything about being a leader, nor did I think about what the term meant. Instead, my main concern was making sure my brothers and sisters were safe, fed, properly dressed, and attending school.

I was not a leader outside my household; that would come later. However, the lessons I absorbed while helping my siblings carried over into my current position at EDCSPIN. At the agency, I'm responsible for more than 500 employees. I don't have to see that they are fed or properly dressed, although their safety is still important to me. My primary focus is on trying to encourage all of them to work with me toward the goal of helping our clients.

There's no single way to accomplish that; anyone who supervises other people knows this. Different approaches must be used to achieve the same goal. I learned that while trying to convince a sibling to behave: Cajoling worked with one, angry looks with another. I picked up more techniques through trial and error and from imitating others I saw in leadership positions: college administrators, the district attorney, elected officials during my stint as a lobbyist, and now from board members at the agency.

The main point is that I have to accept responsibility as the leader, guiding my staff in both form and context. I have to do what is right and appropriate, which encourages my staff to follow suit. At the same time, I have to conduct myself within ethical and legal standards. If I fall short, I must acknowledge my mistake.

None of this happens in isolation. As I mentioned before, the core values of a leader are based on his or her integrity; namely, that part of an individual that no one knows in detail but that everyone hopes is good, positive, and moral. The core of this integrity depends on trust. When signs of shortcomings are observed, distrust becomes the reality. Top leaders attain enduring success and prominence through professional will and personal humility, all the while understanding that criticism serves as a feedback loop to guide them in achieving still more.

I also learned that leadership doesn't come with days off. Great leaders have a full-time mentality that takes them to a higher level of achievement. Great leaders make a full commitment to their company, organization, school, community, country, and other relevant affiliations. Great leaders are fully engaged.

Another thing I learned is that not everyone can be a leader. Leadership doesn't come just from outside factors; it must also come from within. While we can't all be leaders, we can all be motivated, hardworking, and responsible adults.

The secret is motivation. And I've learned a variety of ways to encourage and motivate my staff.

Praise: A Group Worthy of Loyalty

Recognition and rewards is one area that is often overlooked in organizations. People are expected to do their jobs and to perform to the best of their ability, and while that's the ideal, it's also not reality. Some people naturally work hard and are self-motivated, but many others need a push. Occasional compliments go a long way toward keeping someone focused on her job. After all, everyone needs a pat on the back and a word of praise.

Nothing complicated is required; just send a note or maybe some flowers. That's the underlying theme behind such holidays as Administrative Professionals Day, Boss's Day, and the like. They give an opportunity to thank someone for contributing to the success of the organization. Employee of the Month awards are part of the same process. Good organizations provide these kinds of avenues to recognize and reward employees.

The end result is better, more motivated workers. People who are highly self-motivated may not need a pat on the back, but the rest of us aren't that fortunate. We need encouragement and affirmation to stay positive. Nothing provides a better boost to ego than a compliment. Few of us have such confidence that a compliment has no impact.

In fact, most of us feel like outsiders at one time or another. For example, I felt out of place when I started studying at Lincoln University in Pennsylvania. My parents let me go only because an aunt was attending classes there. The setting was strange, almost alien, because it was rural, not like the big city I was used to. I didn't know anyone, and I really felt inferior. It wasn't that my classmates were smarter, but many came from what appeared to be affluent backgrounds. I couldn't help but feel that they were more sophisticated and experienced than I was. After all, at one point I was commuting 350 miles from my home in Brooklyn to the campus, three days a week, and working the other days simply to pay my tuition and reduce expenses. Life for me in those days was not about spending money, wearing designer clothes, or having a lavish lifestyle.

Little changed when I entered law school. Again, many of my classmates seemed so sure of themselves while I was helping found EDCSPIN, maintaining an internship at night, living independently, and struggling to find the energy to keep up. I knew I was as intelligent as anyone there, but I lacked the broad background my colleagues seemed to have. They fit in; I stood out.

Only later did I realize that they, like me, also felt insecure. We all had to find our place in the world. Sometimes, putting on a mask of confidence helps a person survive until experience creates the real thing. I'd like to think I seemed confident even when I wasn't.

I have never been the type to seek compliments, but during those early days I was very grateful when a professor and, later at the DA's office, a supervisor unexpectedly said nice words about my work. That boosted my confidence and helped me feel that I belonged and had added value. These compliments showed that someone took positive notice of what I was doing. Most of us work hard with little feedback, positive or negative. That doesn't motivate anyone.

In fact, a recent Gallup poll found that among workers who really hate their jobs, 57 percent said they were ignored at work.[1] A timely word of genuine appreciation and admiration could reverse that situation for many people. If no one seems to care if you exist, it's hard for you to concentrate on doing your job to the best of your ability. We all need to feel we are part of the larger company and making a contribution, however small.

At EDCSPIN, I make sure that every employee receives some kind of feedback on a regular basis. They need to know I care. They also need to be aware that I am aware of what they are doing and that their contribution to the success of the agency matters. Through these moments of feedback, they realize I am watching them. That's really motivating, as I know; the agency's board of directors watches me. They, in turn, are watched by state regulators. None of us exists in isolation, like a lone fish in a bowl.

Attention like this builds loyalty. By the way, this is not

a popular approach these days. In fact, in many ways, I am bucking a trend. Companies today have moved away from the model of loyalty to the employee and the employee's loyalty to the organization. No one sticks around to get fifty-year pins anymore. The Japanese were once famous for "cradle to grave" employment—not anymore. Few businesses follow that approach. It's just too expensive to continually give raises and boost benefits. Companies now typically hire workers for limited projects and then jettison them.

I'm reminded of a *Doonesbury* cartoon where a boss tells a colleague that he intends to fire everyone and hire them back as contract employees. He cites the millions in savings. His colleague bubbles enthusiastically over the idea and suggests that "we" could really boost the bottom line.

The boss turns to his colleague and says simply, "We?"

The "everyone is replaceable" syndrome undermines loyalty. It may be a necessary business model in certain conditions, but it's hardly motivating. Compliments go a long way to reduce the fear and ease the pain of such an approach, and so does the addition of perks—an assigned parking spot, coupons for meals, or other simple incentives. Such initiatives should not be undertaken in a cynical effort to manipulate, but rather as a sincere effort to reward employees deserving of recognition. Empty compliments are quickly recognized and can reduce motivation. Large recognitions like raises are always welcome, but even a small gesture is greatly appreciated.

Fair Treatment:
Our Work Is About Others

When I was in college, I expected to be treated fairly, no matter how I was dressed or looked. Many times I arrived in class looking unorganized, arriving straight from an impromptu stay at a friend's apartment or from a long commute, but professors did not seem to notice. I would have been upset if they had. Fairness is part of American culture. We Americans do not like it when people cut in line ahead of us to join a friend or seem to take an unfair advantage. We expect everyone to be treated the same. The idea is enshrined in the Declaration of Independence: "All men are created equal."

It took this country a while for the concept to achieve reality. As we all know, slavery ensured that a portion of society was definitely not equal. Women, too, had to fight for their rights, right along with the disabled and gay members of the American family. Those battles continue, although we are definitely closer to achieving equality in many areas.

But those changes came from attitude as well as legislation. The 1964 Civil Rights Act and other national laws helped guarantee the backing of legal authorities if discrimination occurs. At the same time, the emergence of popular Black, gay, and disabled athletes, movie actors, political figures, and other leaders has helped ease the stigmas such persons often confront.

For me, this has meant that I have not run into many of

the same harsh barriers faced by my grandparents and parents. Prejudice still exists and probably always will among some elements of society. Nevertheless, it's not as daunting. With my law degree, for example, I was given the opportunity to pass or fail on my own.

That same concept of equality has to be part of an organization. People have to see that they have a chance to achieve promotions, raises, and other symbols of success based on merit and not on connections or whims. That's reflected in the rewards, as I mentioned in the previous section. Distribution of awards and prizes must be seen as fair in order for them to have any effect or meaning. Bosses who reward only their "pets" quickly generate resentment. Without question, favoritism undermines everything any organization is trying to achieve.

Admittedly, fairness is not perfect. There are a few positions that cannot be available to everyone. For example, a disabled person might have problems with the physical demands of being a firefighter, but there's no reason someone in a wheelchair can't work on the administrative side of that career.

The more an organization looks to merit as a reward criterion, the more employees will work to demonstrate that they deserve such recognition. People who do not feel they have an opportunity because of extraneous conditions quickly lose their motivation for hard work. Fairness also requires that each employee have specific and measurable responsibilities.

I can't criticize a faulty effort if a worker doesn't know what he was supposed to do in the first place.

Placement: Workers Aligned Properly

I strongly believe that anyone who can help another should see it as a privilege and should answer that call. That's why I cofounded EDCSPIN and eventually became its CEO. This turned out to be the right place for me.

We all need to find the best vehicle for our skills and interests. A manager's responsibility is to put an employee in a place where he can achieve the best results.

I don't hire a ballerina to fix the plumbing, for example. If I need someone to use an oar properly, I don't look for someone who knows only how to build a boat. As an attorney, I found that my forte was in developing strategy and arguing in court, not gathering information. The district attorney recognized where my talents lay and allowed me to shine in the area I was strongest.

I take that same approach with my agency. Some people might not be good social workers. They may not enjoy working with clients or have the patience necessary to aid disabled clients with severe needs. However, they may be superb at arranging for treatment and identifying resources. They can be vital members of a team by contributing where they can help the most and achieve personal satisfaction at the same time.

And after all, the alternative isn't pretty. Employees who are misplaced can burn out, get bored, or resent being forced to learn a job they have no interest in.

The process has to begin with interviewing. People regularly apply for positions they are not qualified for simply because they need a job or because they think the opening sounds interesting. But here are some things to look for to make sure that the people you hire are really the best fit for the position:

- The candidate doesn't know key terms or information he or she should know, based on previous experiences.
- The candidate supplies references that are not former employers but colleagues.
- The candidate talks in generalities rather than specifics related to prior job experiences.

To increase our chances of choosing the right candidate, I developed a checklist of what I want the ideal candidate to be able to do. I set the standards for minimal qualifications. That narrows down the list of possible candidates because a large agency like EDCSPIN can have hundreds of applicants for one opening. I want to be sure only the best-qualified candidates actually get into my office for an interview.

I conduct very thorough interviews. I'm looking not only at qualifications and ability but also at whether the candidate fits into the agency's culture. That's more important than many people realize. A brusque person, for example, may cause dissension in an agency where people are considerate of one another.

If I am thorough, I may find someone ill suited for the position she applied for but perfect for another position she had not considered. My goal is to have the best employees working together toward a common goal, paddling together in the same direction, toward the same destination. That's all.

Some companies actually move employees around on a regular basis in hopes of finding the ideal landing spot. Brown & Brown, a large insurance company, employs that strategy. Apparently it works; the company continues to grow.

Handle Complaints: Listen to Everybody

Every now and then one of my brothers and sisters would grumble to me about something. They expected me to respond. Personally, I don't like complaining, but I gradually began to understand why my siblings chose that method of expression. They had concerns and, occasionally, objections. Without a valid route to express their concerns, they groused. Many times they got what they wanted because I—and probably most people—really dislike listening to complaints.

Their grumbling came naturally, as it turns out. Dr. Charles Smith, a Kansas State University professor who specializes in parent-child relationships, says that whining is instilled in childhood: "Children whine because they have learned that kind of repetitious, aggravating behavior gets them what they want. Parents have to realize they created this behavior and now they're going to have to suffer through it."[2] Those of us in the same boat have to suffer as well.

My employees are no different from my siblings in this regard. They are real people who occasionally don't like what they are seeing or are forced to do for their job, and as a result they start complaining. Having seen and heard my share of complainers, I have learned some ways to deal with them that don't include abject surrender in frustration. I'm not suggesting that my approach will work for everyone who grouses, but it has certainly helped at EDCSPIN. Not surprisingly, the same method can work with employees who have unpleasant attitudes.

- ◇ *Don't waste time listening.* I am the boss, so I can say I'm not interested. Colleagues of a constant complainer just need to politely excuse themselves. Complainers abhor silence. They want to vent, and they need an audience for that.
- ◇ *Give credit.* People may grumble because they are looking for attention. They don't necessarily want a raise, but, as noted earlier, employees love recognition for quality work. This isn't a case of the

"squeaky wheel getting the grease," but, as noted earlier, a need for real recognition for a strong effort.

◇ *Make sure an employee knows his future possibilities within the company.* Employees need to understand what the company goals are and why certain actions were taken to align with those goals. They can see what part they play and how their actions affect others. That tends to reduce whining and increase focus.

◇ *Good communication is always significant.* I'll expand on the critical need for good communication in the next chapter.

◇ *When the complaint is job related, try understanding what the concern is really about.* There actually may be something of value behind the grousing. Employees may be reluctant to approach their supervisor or put an objection in writing. Sometimes, a simple explanation will suffice to stifle a grumble. I often hold group meetings to provide explanations for decisions, acknowledging when there are concerns. A side benefit is that employees may raise good points or propose modifications that improve the original idea. I never hesitate to encourage employees to offer their suggestions or to accept those that are plausible or doable. Then, employees want the plan to succeed as much as I do.

◇ *Use humor if possible.* Music may or may not calm the savage beast, but humor can certainly counter bad attitudes. It can be injected through informal discussions.

Remember not to stereotype people who constantly complain. Complainers come in all shapes and sizes. As a result, they cannot all be silenced the same way. For example, some make excuses for everything. To counter them, don't allow excuses. That was the policy in law school. It didn't matter why an assignment was submitted late. After all, courts set deadlines, and those deadlines have to be met. That's true on any job. This way, employees learn to let a supervisor know when there is a problem that may cause a delay. That opens communication channels often blocked by whining.

I doubt that grousing can be completely eliminated. Even the best, most motivated employees may find something they don't like. On the other hand, some people just complain about everything. A company needs to provide avenues through which all employees may raise concerns without recrimination. For people who automatically say no, the response is similar: Ask them for their suggestions and ideas. It's easy to complain; it's harder to provide alternatives. As a result, I often tell my staff: "Don't bring me the problem—bring me the solution."

I also attack complaining from another perspective. I try to eliminate the reasons for the grumbles. This is a multi-step process.

1. *Every employee gets a clear definition of his or her job requirements.* Each of my social workers knows how many hours she is expected to work and other aspects of her job. She knows this before she is offered the job. That helps curtail complaints, since elements of any job can be difficult or annoying. Employees know what is expected; therefore, there's no reason to complain. Besides, if an employee can come up with a better way to do her job, I'm ready to listen.

2. *Each employee knows precisely what he or she is accountable for.* Every time she visits a client, she must turn in a report. There are regular meetings with supervisors to discuss progress, problems, and plans. The lines of communication remain open so that any problems are addressed before the employee turns to grumbling in order to be heard.

3. *Adopt an open-door/open-discussion policy.* Employees are not punished for coming to see me about a concern. I always include their supervisor in any decision. As a result, everyone is welcomed and stays on the same page. This started when I

arrived in 2007. Some members of the previous administration did not allow the free flow of information from the staff to the director and back. Oftentimes, it was a one-way street. Unfortunately, that often led to information traffic jams, confusion, and unproductivity.

4. *Address employee concerns; each person is naturally concerned first and foremost about him- or herself.* Regardless of how petty a complaint may seem, it's not petty to the employee who raised it. For example, when we needed to replace the carpet in the agency, employees at all levels were involved in picking the color and even the style. This is called a "buy-in." The employees bought into the process because they were part of it.

5. *Reduce stress.* This is a really serious problem in American business, where 90 percent of employees complain about excess stress. Much of that comes from their feeling of a lack of control over their circumstances. The best answer is to get employees involved not just in decisions but also in understanding the direction the company wants to go and why.

As with most things, clear and open communication reduces complaints, leaving grumblers with nothing to moan about. Often, though, the complaints really aren't about a boss or some element of the job. Instead, the problem may be the job itself. After all, some people were not cut out to use an oar, but would make great navigators or coxswains. As noted earlier, the key is to put people where they can use their natural abilities to the organization's greatest advantage.

Setting a Good Example: Leadership Without Leaders

Throughout my life, I have enjoyed performing in track-and-field events. Today, I go skydiving and compete in marathons. I don't just tell employees to try to stay in shape and keep active; I actually do something about it by practicing what I preach.

I also want my employees to see how we must work together by having them participate in agency decisions. For me, this embodies what Dr. King meant when he said, "Leadership and followership go hand in hand." The civil rights icon also used to say that a genuine leader is not a searcher for consensus but a molder of consensus.

It takes a person of great integrity and perseverance to see what is needed in society and decide to lead change. As Dr. King said, "If we are to go forward, we must go back and rediscover those precious values—that all reality hinges on moral foundations and that all reality has spiritual control."[3]

I believe I am succeeding. A nonprofit developer once said

that I am a "thought-provoking visionary who speaks from his experience and humble beginnings that have allowed him to be a firm yet compassionate leader who sets an example for those around him." That example is about dedication, commitment, and hard work. I am in my office early in the morning and on weekends, and I stay late. If I expect my staff to give their all, I must be willing to do the same. EDCSPIN employees can't miss that model.

Anyone in a leadership position can do the same thing.

◆　◆　◆

Throughout my career, I have come across people whose experiences have empowered and inspired me. Stacie Henderson is one of those people. So, I decided to write her story because it must be told; extraordinary people's experiences are worth knowing. Her commitment to excellence explains her rise to prominence in the intensely competitive world of high-fashion marketing and retail. Her experience illuminates the ways that a gifted, self-aware leader can focus a team's efforts to achieve lofty goals in a high-pressure environment, then refocus and recalibrate those same abilities to move a new team in an entirely new direction.

PERSPECTIVE: TIRELESS VISIONARY—STACIE HENDERSON,

U.S. HEAD OF E-COMMERCE AND DIGITAL AT TOD'S GROUP; CO-FOUNDER, FASHION TECH CONNECTS; BOARD MEMBER, FASHION SCHOLARSHIP FUND; CDFA BLACK ADVISORY BOARD

Charles A. Montorio-Archer

The "Everybody Paddles" mission is meant to inspire people to work at the same time, in the same direction, toward the same goal. The mission requires a team effort and implies that no one can be left behind. But what happens when those goals have been attained, when there is seemingly nowhere left to paddle? Sometimes we may believe that this point has been reached—until an immense opportunity presents itself.

Take Stacie Henderson's experience, for example. She is the quintessential polished professional. Soon after obtaining a master's degree in fashion management from SDA Bocconi (a Triple Crown Business School), she focused her talents on creative marketing strategies for the luxury brand Salvatore Ferragamo SPA in Florence, Italy. Before she was able to truly fulfill her role there, she had to acquaint herself with the Italian culture. After becoming fluent both linguistically and culturally, Henderson strengthened the Ferragamo Parfums fragrance portfolio in the Japanese market by overseeing the strategic marketing of a new fragrance, Incanto Dream. The success of her strategy resulted in the global rollout of the fragrance. Henderson's dedication and vision for the brand led her to the position of global marketing director. With a wealth of experience and a firm grasp on consumer-trends research, Henderson decided it was time to paddle forward.

In February 2006, Henderson returned to the United States and began a new role as director of marketing for the international luxury brand Versace in New York City. Wasting no time, she developed marketing programs that targeted micro-segmentation of potential customers, aggressive product-focused media plans, and vital collaborations with key organizations. As a part of the executive team, Henderson developed marketing strategies that supported sales for both the retail and the wholesale divisions. She was part of a dynamic executive team that witnessed double-digit growth for the brand. Henderson continued her eminence and sharpened her focus by implementing social media and email marketing strategies to enhance Versace's global presence, which brought about a triple-digit database increase. Her dedication, drive, and fearlessness in taking the plunge into digital efforts with Versace played an instrumental role in her promotion to vice president of marketing and events.

With all of these achievements and a solid international network of high-end fashion industry professionals, what more could she have wanted? During a recent interview, she spoke candidly about her time at Versace.

"I loved everything about my job. There was nothing about it that I disliked, but I knew that I wanted something that would challenge me, constantly . . . I realized that sometimes you have to take a chance and try something new that provides you a new set of challenges. I still keep in touch with my Versace family. I learned so much from my time there."

Henderson found her new set of challenges when she was contacted regarding a position with the U.S. unit of the Westfield Group as vice president of marketing for the Westfield World Trade Center. "When I was told that I had the opportunity to be instrumental in changing the landscape of downtown Lower Manhattan," she said, "I realized this was a pretty big deal."

Westfield oversees retail operations for a 350,000-square-foot shopping and dining complex at the World Trade Center site. This is the first New York City undertaking for Westfield, which initially acquired the rights to the WTC retail complex in 2001. Adding this latest enhancement to its global retail real estate portfolio, Westfield has designed a space that will hold 150 shops (fashion, dining, services, and others), and Stacie Henderson manages the brand positioning, advertising, digital outreach, public relations, and tourism for the new retail district.

And Henderson's vision is broader than the formidable business opportunities involved in the undertaking. "The beauty is, we are looking at this as the rebirth, the revitalization of this area." As an integral part of the Westfield team, Henderson has already started the process of creating the tightest possible focus for her target consumer audience. Her primary objective is to work with her team to create a destination that will top the must-see lists of New Yorkers and visitors alike.

Henderson is steadfast in her vision for this retail space. While recognizing that rebuilding downtown Manhattan is a huge endeavor, she is sure that the team she has become a part of will paddle in the same direction, unified in their goal to make this all possible. As she asserts: "It is truly a collective undertaking, and my company is a part of it. There are several organizations that will come together to make this project instrumental to the revival of downtown Manhattan . . . If people walk in and we can surprise and delight them the moment they come through the door—if we can exceed their expectations and give them a great experience—my vision for this space will be fulfilled."

PERSPECTIVE: MISSION-DRIVEN TEAMING

Jacki Davidoff, Chief Potential Officer, and John Davidoff,
Chief Mission Driver, Davidoff Strategy

Relationships are messy. We learned this the hard way. A coach pointed out in our seventh year of marriage that we were in a conflict-avoidant relationship. What? We felt it was a virtue that we never fought. We have since learned that not fighting, not expressing our true feelings, and not saying our truths to one another were all barriers to us developing more cohesion and more closeness as a couple. We were also missing the primary benefit of being on a team: creating opportunities for each person to learn and grow as we relate to each other, react to each other, and take risks to be more real with each other.

With the support and structure of twenty-plus years in a couples program offered by the Wright Foundation for the Realization of Human Potential, we started on a journey of learning and growing in our own teaming through our marriage. Our team has raised and launched two young adults, managed a household, and participated in community—through membership in faith communities, politics, and volunteering with nonprofit organizations. Perhaps this was all training for the next level of teaming we took on, when we decided to work together in our family-owned consulting, leadership coaching, and training company.

Teaming in a relationship—whether at work with colleagues, with a significant other, with family and friends, or those in community—is an amazing opportunity to tap the potential in ourselves that has yet to be tapped. This is the gift of *Mission-Driven Teaming*. In *Mission-Driven Teaming*, each member of the team is learning more about who they can become. It takes opening yourselves to others on the team, and being aware of what you are learning from your fear, hurts, anger, sadness, and joy. Being open, and trusting yourself and others can lead to exceptional self-development and strengthening the team at the same time. As this upward trajectory in the potency of each member of the Mission-Driven team is happening, the team is discovering that it can achieve greater results toward its goals and objectives for being a team.

Any relationship has spoken and unspoken contracts. When we said our wedding vows to one another, we promised to help one other become their best self. That was our spoken contract. Examples of our unspoken contracts were: I won't give you trouble if you don't give me trouble, or I will provide security for you if you don't challenge me to be someone I don't want to be. We created a nice relationship from not having said the truth of all our expectations of one another. We later learned that our relationship was missing higher levels of trust, engagement, intention, commitment, and responsibility. We were, in fact, living the antithesis of our marriage vows of helping the other become their best selves. We were actually limiting each other's development. In holding ourselves back from being real, we were creating a culture of holding our team back. We see this often in our consulting with hundreds of organizations, boards, and teams. When teams tiptoe around each other, they take the team down to the lowest common denominator of aliveness and performance and satisfaction.

Mission-Driven teaming is a way of life. It leads to personal and organizational transformation, where the possibility of what a team can achieve is increasingly expanded. We have experienced this in our own company as we have achieved a national reputation for our work supporting organizations to drive mission through strategic planning, leadership development, and creating high-performing cultures. We are also privileged to witness our clients' leaders and organizations make challenging shifts toward *Mission-Driven Teaming*, such as expecting more from one another, eliminating drama (e.g., shame, blame, and justification) from the culture, taking individual risks with one another, establishing learning and growing as an organization value, and learning the skill of fighting for the organizations and the people it serves.

We have learned that growth mindsets are essential for *high* functioning and satisfied teams and team members, even [especially] in a committed relationship. With growth mindsets, each member of the team focuses on the positive aspects of the team, minimizing the negative aspects. Mission-Drivers are also 100% responsible for their satisfaction being on the team. They presume good faith with the other team members.[4] We have practiced these agreements in our marriage as well as in our business. We learned these teaming agreements from our own leadership coaches, Drs. Bob and Judith Wright, cofounders of the Wright Foundation for the Realization of Human Potential (www.WrightFoundation.org). Through coaching and participating in a group with other couples, we have been on a lifelong journey to learn to integrate and harness these agreements. Having outside support is an essential part of being on a Mission-Driven team. As our clients use us for individual leadership coaching and for training leadership teams toward enhancing their Mission-Driven culture, we would not be authentic Mission-Driven team members if we did not also invest in coaching for us as a couple and for our company.

Remember, relationships are messy. If you are not having conflict, moments of wanting to trash your team members, or ill will for the burden of sharing responsibility for the team's outcomes, then you are probably not yet on the field where Mission-Driven teaming happens. It's not always pretty, but with training in *Mission-Driven Teaming* skills, it can become a transformational experience where you look back and realize you and the team are not the same people as when you started. *Mission-Driven Teaming* is not an outcome. It is a way of choosing to live in every area of your professional and personal life. We feel blessed in being students and teachers of the *Mission-Driven Teaming* way of life. We hope to have our team cross paths with your team out there in this wondrous world of Mission-Drivers.

PERSPECTIVE: TRENCH LEADERSHIP

Mark Dhooge, President and CEO of
Kids In Distress and Family Central

The first and most significant memory that flashes through my head as a young athlete is a vivid recollection of Coach Koski running beside me during the very last drill of a grueling high school football practice. Coach would repeatedly tell me, "Mark, if you don't dig deep, no one else will. As one of the leaders of this team, YOU need to set the pace." We were tired, exhausted, and spent, yet Coach was running there right beside us, just like he did during every drill, every sprint, and every exercise, right up to the moment that we all thought he was going to make us pass out from exhaustion. He always demonstrated that we had more in us than we thought—and when it came to hard work, he was the first to jump in and start the calisthenics. I remember the last game we played, running down the open field and catching a glimpse out of the corner of my eye of the man who poured the foundation of my leadership philosophy, running down the sidelines "with" me, clipboard in hand. I learned very early through the mentorship and modeling of Coach Koski that to truly motivate, mentor, and inspire your team, you must dig right along with them; respect is earned though participating and running alongside your team. And, if getting dirty, sweaty, exhausted, and falling down is beneath you, then leadership is beyond you.

I had no idea at that time how impactful those football practices would be to the formation of my personal values and leadership principles. To this day I've studied a lot of leaders, coaches, and visionaries; however, I have not yet met a man or woman who worked harder to lead by example and who led with his head and his heart—not with his ego—than Coach.

It is a leadership style often referred to as "trench leadership." Trench leadership is not often talked about in mainstream leadership books, classes, or seminars, but I believe it is the most important. It is the behavior, modeling, and work that is found in the trenches, where some of the hardest battles of corporate alignment and company culture are fought. It is the leadership that will inspire the next generation of team members to do daring things in the face of adversity.

Trench leadership requires us as leaders to BE ready so that we do not need to GET ready. The philosophy requires that we are able to lead ourselves before leading others, by constantly gaining knowledge, by learning and knowing every aspect of our business, and by carefully and meticulously formulating plans with involvement in mind. If you cannot lead yourself, how can you ever expect to lead others? If you cannot motivate yourself to prepare for an upcoming business meeting, have an organized documentation structure, or lay out an intricate sales protocol, how can you expect any of your colleagues to respect your leadership? You must be the living embodiment of what your team aspires to be; you must lead by example. You must get in that trench and dig right alongside them.

The decision to engage in trench leadership with your people can be both a bold and vulnerable step toward the leadership development of your team. I have found that leading in the trenches will empower some folks, while filling others with the nervousness of "the boss being here." Consistency is key. It requires the consistency of disciplined thought along with disciplined action, which will act as an accelerant for the team's success. This consistency will instill and build confidence in the team. It is a well-established fact that courage begets courage. As such, your teams are more likely to make their own tough decisions, take responsibility for those decisions, and own their assigned portion of the business when you model the way of thinking and acting you would like to see displayed around you.

A year ago, at the onset of the COVID-19 pandemic, our organization, Kids In Distress, launched a food, diaper, and backpack distribution to assist those folks in our community who had been hit hard economically by the crisis. We had the collaborative partners in place, the space and resources to hold the distribution, and the vehicles to deliver these much-needed items to families in the community. Unfortunately, there was also an undeniable problem, fear. Our team was fearful of being exposed to COVID-19. Very early on, we set the stage that all leaders, including me, the CEO, and Tony, our CFO, would be assisting with the distribution. We blocked off the three-hour time frame on our calendars each Monday to assist with the sorting, packing, and loading of the pallets of emergency food and diapers that were being placed in trunks or delivered to families with no transportation. We furnished our entire team with personal protective equipment for the initiative at hand. We all "dug deep" even during the hottest days of July and August to ensure that the five hundred-plus families who were relying on us each week had food in their homes. The initiative was a huge leadership success. Yes, we were feeding thousands of people; however, the win was also demonstrated within our team. The distribution became a success that the entire agency rallied around, bringing us all closer together during this unprecedented crisis. It mattered not if you were in the agency housekeeping department, preschool, executive offices, or board room, everyone paddled, as Charles would say, and as a result our agency culture took a huge leap forward.

Which also begets the statement: *Leading from the trench is not for the faint of heart.* It can be demanding, time consuming, and downright dangerous. As a trench leader, your very core must be consumed with investing in the next generation of young leaders, and you must be willing to spend AND be spent, in order to obtain a return on that investment. Trench leaders are not afraid to "get dirty" with their people even if it requires:

- Making major commitments of time
- Serving without recognition
- Placing emotions out where they can be damaged
- Investing in programs others see as not worthy
- Subjecting yourself to criticism
- Rebuilding and redirecting young leaders repeatedly
- Sacrificing work–life balance

However, the rewards of trench leadership are much greater than what may be perceived as downsides. Like many other leadership principles, digging in alongside your team should and can be used as a precursor to build on other, more complex leadership practices that require a relationship foundation. There is no greater way to develop the trust required of leaders than to work alongside your team. Team members routinely flock to those leaders who demonstrate themselves as being trustworthy and genuine. They reinforce those values by displaying a commitment to their people by their daily work and actions. I've seen firsthand that it is nearly impossible to establish trust with a team when leaders act as if their power, authority, and/or title allows them to bypass certain tasks, jobs, or activities because they feel "privileged" or above something that may seem menial in nature. Trench leaders embrace every opportunity that allows them to assist their team, whether an easy or a difficult task or assignment.

It is truly within this "togetherness environment" that leaders begin to see the vision for their team manifest itself by the increased confidence, enhanced preparation, knowledge of the project at hand, and establishment of trust that develops through working beside them. People follow leaders initially because they have to, based on title, position, or authority. Trench leaders demonstrate camaraderie, equality, and respect, which evolves the relationship between leader and follower to the extent that people follow based on who the leader is, what the leader has done for them, and what they truly represent.

PERSPECTIVE: ALLIES AND AMBASSADORS

*Dr. Jody Levison–Johnson, President and CEO of both The Alliance for
Strong Families and Communities and The Council on Accreditation*

In 2011, I was recruited to serve in state government and
lead a broad-scale children's behavioral health transformation. This required me to move to a southern state,
which after a lifetime in New York, was a big deal for me
both professionally and personally.

Part of what drew me to the opportunity was the leadership challenge it posed. Revolutionizing the behavioral
health system in one of the nation's poorest states with
some of the worst outcomes would be a tremendous
opportunity—for me, as well as for the residents of the
state. During a conversation with my husband and
me, the leader recruiting me shared that the state was
ranked forty-ninth out of fifty according to one national
organization's assessment of children's well-being. My
husband wondered out loud what ranking she was
hoping for as a result of the transformation, "Like thirty
or something?" She laughed and said, "Actually, I was
thinking more like forty-seven or forty-eight." Mike
replied, "My wife can do that." I realized during that
conversation that it could not get much worse for the
state's residents who were dependent on public sector
behavioral health services. If I could come and offer

any movement that improved the quality of life, then I was making a tremendous contribution. It was a difficult decision after spending my entire life in Rochester, among my friends and family, and successfully climbing the ladder at my current organization where I had been named vice president the year before. As I sat in the hotel room during the visit to meet state leadership and talked it through with Mike, I tearfully and fearfully determined that it was the right move. It posed a bigger challenge than I had ever faced and offered the biggest potential payoff I could ever imagine, impacting the lives of millions who were struggling with behavioral health challenges and were able to access only substandard care.

We moved over Memorial Day weekend in 2011. I remember crying for the first four hours of our journey and doubting my decision. I remember feeling a sense of ominousness and loneliness like I had never felt before. I kept holding on to my rationale for my liberal Jewish, New York self to be moving to the conservative, largely Catholic Deep South. I was in pursuit of better outcomes for the public sector people of this state. And according to Mike, "I could do that." In that twenty-three-hour drive I got to do a lot of thinking. I remember contemplating what my approach would be, given that I had no credibility with nearly anyone in the state and that I was being brought in to do a largely unpopular task. While the administration and I framed this as improving access to and quality of behavioral health services, the child-serving systems and providers viewed it as turning over control of their system to an outsider, initially me, and ultimately to a managed care organization.

Given what I knew about the South, which really was not much at all, I did realize that my fast-talking, know-it-all approach was not going to work. I decided that I needed to focus on two things: listening and relationships. This was a huge leadership challenge for me. While I had honed both of these skills in my work in Rochester, I had not had to fundamentally change my style. Culturally, I could be who I was when I was in Rochester. In this new role, being an expert from the North was not an asset, and I needed to build alliances with people who were untrusting of outsiders. I opened myself to the idea that I had as much to learn as I did to teach and welcomed the experience as one that offered tremendous opportunity not only for the people of the state, but also for me.

I hit the ground running once I arrived. As part of the way to build cross-system buy-in, the team I had been assigned to support the effort was comprised of representatives from several state agencies—Behavioral

Health, Medicaid, Child Welfare, Juvenile Justice, and Education. Each of the people on the team had different levels of understanding of what we intended to accomplish; different philosophies on how to achieve the best outcomes for children, youth, and families; and different overarching mandates. When I arrived, the team had been extensively and exclusively focused on the regulatory and financing aspects of the shift. These components were not my forte and in all honestly were not at all energizing. They were necessary aspects to our effort but didn't result in a sense of shared ownership or a source of excitement. Breeding passion and energy for a team of relatively disconnected strangers seemed to be the most critical aspect to launching the effort across this unaligned team.

And so we got to work, focusing on the values and principles that were the foundation of our efforts. We talked about notions of being strength-based, community-based, family driven, youth guided, and culturally competent. We talked about the big downstream impacts of helping young people and their families feel more connected to each other and their communities. And we talked about being the army of ambassadors to combat the lines that had been drawn between each of the child-serving systems, between these systems and the families who were served by them, and between the provider agencies and the families who received services in their organizations. We bred a sense of shared commitment and a shared vision.

Within a few weeks of settling into my apartment and working with this team, I was on a statewide tour with the deputy secretary to share our ideas and start to garner support. Using the values and principles that our team had embraced, I held fast to the assertion that we were seeking to make things better for the people of state and shared experiences from across the country where similar efforts had led to three things: people getting better, people being satisfied, and costs being reduced.

This was my bipartisan approach to garnering support for the three and half years that I was there. I faced many hostile environments where I was reminded that this state was different and faced different challenges that I could not possibly know or understand. Through it all, I listened. I validated people's experiences and tried to join and engage and develop relationships. This was not easy, and without the support of the deputy secretary and my army of ambassadors, I may have packed up and headed home. They repeatedly reminded me that I had something to offer and had been brought there for a reason. As natives to the state, they forged fearlessly into their respective home departments and every forum and did their best to share our message and lend me their credibility.

At times the listening I had committed to was hard for me. People told stories of extreme outliers that challenged what we were trying to establish: a broad spectrum of community-based alternatives that would allow people to remain in their homes and communities instead of in institutions. They shared scenarios that quite honestly may never have happened but were painted as clear evidence that people needed to be locked up to get treated for behavioral health issues. Through at times gritted teeth, I listened. I validated. I attempted to join. I also introduced new ideas and different lenses by which we could view things. Subtly and over time, I seeded the state with people who were at least willing to question the status quo. Those people became my allies and my ambassadors. They became my cultural brokers who helped pave the way for new ideas with people and in places that were firmly entrenched in antiquated approaches. We made headway. We had the backing of the governor who, despite differing from me in so many ways, was supportive of our efforts.

As I look back on these experiences, I see fundamental ties between how I approached this work and my own continued progression to be increasingly aware of not only the power dimensions of leadership, but also the importance of followers and their needs. It ties to my shift to be more concerned about the collaborative process and impact on a group (or groups) versus simply my own needs and aspirations.

As I considered whether to take the job and for the years I was there, I was committed to being values-based. I consistently grounded any conversation in my values and philosophy, expressed these from my perspective as clearly as possible, and did my best to deliver on commitments. Each time I sat down with key partners, I started the conversation with establishing common ground, that we were all committed to improving the quality of supports and services available for young people with behavioral health conditions and their families. I shared that together we could envision a time when the state would have what was needed to do right by its residents, creating and inspiring a shared vision. I would then speak about the idea of less reliance on institutional services and more community-based service offerings. I would illustrate these concepts with data that allowed people to move away from the status quo based on evidence. And as I shared, these efforts resulted in people understanding and ultimately becoming champions for this new way of being. As I honestly reflect on my work there and how I approached it, I realize that as the captain, I set the course, but the whole crew—which included my team at the state and the countless system leaders, providers, families, young people, and other partners—paddled to lead us through our systemic reform effort.

PERSPECTIVE: LEADER, KNOW THYSELF

Armani Scott, Father, Filmmaker, Writer, Attorney

Ask yourself the question, "What is MY Leadership Style?" and you may be opened up to revelation knowledge and personal growth.

Before anyone can hope to *effectively* lead others, they must first be able to *govern themselves*: a) to *exercise humility*, receive instruction, and accept the leadership of others; b) to *practice integrity*, holding themselves to a standard of doing what is right whether or not someone else is watching; and c) to *ask themselves all the hard questions and give honest answers.*

Humility – Before a leader commands the respect of her team, she must *acknowledge the purpose of leadership in action*, recognize the leadership of another, be a good team member herself, and watch someone else lead so she may learn and grow wise.

Integrity – Before a leader demands the loyalty of her team, she will lead herself, appreciate the impact of unquestioned leadership, and learn how each team member's individual integrity enhances and strengthens the team.

Authenticity – Before a leader can look her team in the eye and enroll their full, enthusiastic effort, she must look herself in the eye, being critically transparent with herself so when she stands before her team, the truths she speaks to them have been first spoken to herself.

Know Thyself

What is my leadership style?

The consistent, intentional act of *introspection* will heighten your awareness, enhancing and empowering your perception.

As applied to the concept of effective leadership, your *heightened awareness* (to truly know thyself) has a myriad of benefits.

If the *benefits of heightened awareness* are not readily apparent to you, take some time to meditate on the notion of what it would be like to have the *superpower of awareness*: imagine what you could accomplish if you were more *aware* of the universe and all your surroundings, *including the people you interact with on a daily basis.* Think about what you're thinking about. Consider what you are aware of—and not . . . then continue.

A leader may be more aware of her own strengths and weaknesses—what aspects of her personality to develop and promote—as well as the parts of her character where she requires correction and support, places to get better.

She may see herself from the perspective of others and with awareness not only of her own position but of the positions of those around her who project confidence.

A leader who is aware might better recognize the strengths and weaknesses of her team members; she may even be more thoughtful about the best ways to encourage strengths and provide corrective instruction.

A leader who is aware may empathize with her team.

Through empathy, she can create a powerful, symbiotic bond with the team she leads. She will have placed herself in the shoes of her team members, and from her position of leadership maintains AWARENESS of her team's needs. Her team then intuitively responds in kind to the needs and directives of their leader.

Imagine yourself a confident leader:

Iron will (confidence) tempered by truest empathy.

Build authentic, honest, genuine confidence from within. Give the same decency and respect you desire for yourself to those who lead you and those you lead. Project genuine confidence and true empathy to your team from a place of AUTHENTIC AWARENESS, and get everyone to agree.

COMMUNICATE CLEARLY TO STAY ON COURSE

I learned in dramatic fashion about the importance to leaders of clear communication. By the time I was working as a lobbyist in Albany, New York, in 2007, I had taken several courses in communication, through which I learned all the appropriate theories. But as I continued my work within the legislative process to obtain funds for social service agencies around the state, I soon discovered that the theory and the practice of communication were drastically different undertakings.

At that time, I was also on the board of EDCSPIN. Since I lived far away in Albany, my role at the nonprofit was limited to reviewing decisions made by the executive director, approving grants, and the like. When I could be on-site, I also enjoyed providing some input into the agency through mentoring, team-building exercises, training in presentation techniques, as well as modeling professional etiquette.

Imagine my dismay, then, to learn that there were major problems at EDCSPIN. I was stunned and disappointed. On top of that, because of my experience as a lobbyist in the state capital, I was asked to take the reins of our social service agency.

I was hesitant. For one thing, the current executive director was very popular, as I saw during my infrequent visits to the agency. The staff liked him, and they were not going to be happy he was leaving. Then, too, I knew that some would speculate that I, as a founding board member, had somehow orchestrated his exit. Any change in leadership excites similar imaginary motives and generates conspiracy theories. Finally, there was the problem of getting the employees to focus on our clients, not on internal personnel matters.

Thus, I was faced with a real communication problem with multiple facets. After a lot of thinking and discussions with friends, I decided to take the job. I then spent a lot of time working out a communication strategy. I needed to calm the staff while, at the same time, maintaining their loyalty to the agency. I also had to ease any concerns our clients might have had and at the same time convince regulatory agencies that EDCSPIN was back on track.

I had little experience dealing with this kind of an emergency. It wasn't like finding a Band-Aid for an injured sibling or figuring out how to come up with the money for tuition. I had handled those problems my entire life. This problem cut across so many more boundaries than anything I had faced before.

Large corporations often hire public relations companies that provide guidance during testing times in an organization's life. I didn't have that luxury. Besides, adding an outsider to the mix would only have increased confusion. I needed to show that I was in charge and could handle the complex situation. What I said mattered; how I appeared mattered even more. As I will discuss in more detail a bit later, many times tacit communication can be just as important as anything spoken or written.

In this situation, success depended on combining each element to win over a skeptical staff. I could not be afraid to fail. At other points in my life I had failed, but I knew that the secret in such circumstances is to get back up, brush off the "dust" of a sense of failure or humiliation, and keep trying, just as that great tune "Pick Yourself Up" put it so well.[1]

Opening Act: Creating Positive First Impressions

I started by sending email announcements to all staff members requiring them to attend a group meeting the day after the former executive director was scheduled to leave. I also had signs posted on the entrance to announce the meeting. I did not tell anyone what the meeting concerned. After all, grapevines have a way of divulging all the news anyway. I scheduled the meeting before normal working hours to be sure our clients were not shortchanged.

On the day of the meeting, I arrived early. I had purchased donuts on the way to work and waited in my office while employees slowly began to arrive. At the time, the agency was in smaller quarters, so there was only one room big enough for everyone to gather in. Everyone gathered in the main room, which included desks and chairs as well as a coffee machine.

I didn't have to be with them long to know that they were turning on the whine engine full blast. Some employees were "sure" I had engineered a takeover. Others were equally "sure" that the previous director should not have been let go. Everyone traded rumors, ratcheting up emotions along the way.

I did not interfere.

About fifteen minutes before the scheduled meeting, I walked into the room and set out the donuts. I didn't say anything, but I wanted the employees to know I cared about them and about not wasting money, so these weren't fancy. The former executive director used to put out any pastries left over from his meetings, so employees knew what the directors were served; the difference was obvious.

No one spoke to me, although they flocked to the donuts with obvious enthusiasm. Next time, I decided, I'd opt for a healthier snack.

At the exact time set for the meeting, I walked forward and stood in front of the group. Eyes followed me from the moment I stepped through the doorway. Everyone grew quiet. I could sense hostility. Most did not know me. I may have been cofounder of the agency, but I had worked in another city. The board meetings were held after-hours. I recognized only a few faces.

I had left my tie and suit coat in the office. My intent was to demonstrate again without saying anything that I was a working person like them and that I was rolling up my sleeves too. I didn't have to ask for quiet; side conversations had stopped, and everyone was staring at me. I stood in front of them for a moment, calmly counting heads. The pause gave me time to relax. It also allowed them to look at me and register my appearance. The previous director had his own, very individual style that set him off from everyone else. In contrast, my style is to dress like the staff. They knew immediately that things were very different, even before I said anything.

Most of the staffers sat in small clumps, where they had been whispering to one another. Everyone seemed to have a cup of coffee and a donut; the three boxes in the back of the room were already empty.

I smiled. I really can't claim to be personable; my intent was not to make friends, but rather to show that they had a strong leader who was not intimidated by the needs of the moment. They needed to recognize that their jobs were safe and that the agency would not be closing. The calmer I was, the calmer they would be. So, I smiled, and after a moment, I could almost see people relaxing. I knew I had to sound strong, not scared or shaky. Employees would read trouble into my words if they were not clear and confident. I wanted to communicate all of this with my demeanor.

I could almost hear the many questions bubbling just below the surface of the faces watching me. Since I hadn't intended to become the executive director, I had prepared no speech. Instead, I decided to speak from the heart.

"Some of you know me," I said quietly. I did not shout. "For the rest, let me introduce myself. More than a decade ago, I helped start this agency. Some of you know I have been on the board of directors." I paused. Everyone continued to stare. "As of today, I am your chief executive officer." I spoke in a straightforward manner, without a hint that the announcement was anything special.

I could hear the whispers start. Everyone wanted to know what had happened. I did not tell them; that was none of their business. Instead, I assured them that the agency would continue normally. Their positions would be unaffected. I told them that the agency would open its doors at the usual time, and they would resume helping our clients as always. Naturally, that prompted other questions. I answered each one patiently. I was honest, but there were things they did not need to know. I believe strongly in providing the information that employees must have, but that doesn't mean they need every detail. Besides, such nonessential information often gets distorted in the retelling and creates more problems.

Employees learned that their salaries would not drop and that positions would not be affected unless someone was not qualified for the job. I knew—as did everyone else—that the previous director had hired a few friends. They resigned shortly thereafter, which relieved me of the need to fire them. At the first meeting, employees also learned that the state had complete confidence in the agency's ability to fulfill its contracts, and that I did too. They learned that I planned no major changes; that the agency had a strong future; that they were important; and that I cared about their futures. Some of this message was stated; the rest came through in how I spoke and was communicated by my firm, upright stance. They could tell I meant everything I said.

The whole meeting lasted less than fifteen minutes. I deliberately did not leave a lot of time between the end of it and when the agency usually opened. I knew that the staff would get antsy, eager to not fall behind on the work schedule. Thus, in effect, they managed themselves. Besides, not many would have the nerve to speak up at a large meeting. Consequently, I also scheduled a one-on-one meeting with each employee as well as additional group sessions.

I used the large gatherings to stress teamwork. Initially, I relied on the "We are in the same boat" metaphor, and that soon expanded into the "Everybody Paddles" concept.

Meetings with individuals were as short or as long as the person required. Some people wanted to talk; this was not so much to find answers as to ingratiate themselves with me. That did not cloud my judgment. I looked at what they were doing, not how manipulative they were acting.

A few were in positions they were not qualified for. Because they were good workers, however, I was able to shift people around to better match skills to positions. I also needed to demonstrate flexibility. The employees had to know I was not a dictator, that I was a partner in the agency's efforts. I was picking up my paddle, too.

Some of the individual meetings were difficult, to be sure. Several staffers had been hired by the previous director and were very loyal to him. I needed for them to transfer that loyalty to me, and that could happen only with one-on-one conversations where they could see and hear that I shared their enthusiasm for their work and actually knew a lot about it. At the same time, they had to know they did not face any kind of punishment for supporting their former boss. Confidence and knowledge communicate their own strong messages.

Virtually all of those employees wanted to stay and soon began to trust my leadership. But not everyone chose to remain, and when that happened, I understood. Some people were committed to the previous director, and nothing I said or did could change that. I did not reprimand them; I sympathized with their need to make such a life-changing decision and wished them well.

I also tried to help them find new jobs. Because of my lobbying experience, I knew directors at other agencies and was able to locate positions suited to the abilities of some former EDCSPIN employees. Admittedly, I was not unhappy to see them leave, since I knew that the new people I hired would be concerned about pleasing me, not trying to undermine whatever I chose to do.

The most important aspect was to maintain open communication. Employers must communicate often, especially with each other. Alex "Sandy" Pentland, the director of MIT's Human Dynamics Laboratory and the MIT Media Lab Entrepreneurship Program, said that in a "typical project team, a dozen or so communication exchanges per working hour may turn out to be optimum; but more or less than that, and team performance can decline."[2]

Such communication can be broken into three types: tacit, oral, and written. Each type of communication plays an important role in any successful organization.

Tacit: Nonverbal Behavior

As you could see in the scenario I described above, I sent nonverbal messages through such visual cues as the donuts, my clothing, and my manner when standing in front of the employees. My efforts seemed effective, and certainly that approach was better than a written manifesto or some other document.

Dr. Mehmet Oz, a cardiac surgeon and TV guru, says that silent communication methods "are more powerful than we give them credit for. At times, they speak volumes. Far more than even a multitude of words can. What we portray visually, through how we dress, the manner in which we carry ourselves, our nonverbal communiqués—this all sends messages to those around us."[3]

Those messages are important. I've quoted one of my role models several times already, and here, too, I believe Dr. Martin Luther King Jr. provided the best example of using tacit communication that I can think of. When he spoke, he spoke directly and honestly. While his words were important, his audience could see by his manner, even without his words, that he lived what he was saying and would continue to live it after he left the podium or stage. When King stepped in front of an audience, he seemed to electrify everyone there. That connection created an experience rather than simply an event. People tuned in to one another as well as to Dr. King. They were moved to action simply by his presence. I don't want to suggest that everyone has that kind of charisma, but any leader must be aware of the energy of his or her audience and tap into it.

Perhaps the most-studied form of nonverbal communication involves body language. I was well aware of that and made sure that at the initial staff meeting I stood as tall as I could, with my body facing my audience. I'm not a tall person, but thin pants and a straight back help create an illusion of height. When I was asked a question, I turned to face the person asking and answered directly without pause. I kept my hands out of my pockets and tried to present a picture of control.

I wasn't doing anything new. The ancient Greeks understood that how we stand and look displays information, and scholars in the 1600s wrote treatises on hand gestures. In the mid-nineteenth century, evolutionary theorist Charles Darwin also studied body language, yet most people were unaware of the topic until the publication in 1970 of *Body Language* by Julius Fast.

Today there are lists that "decode" body language. For example, frequent blinking denotes excitement or pressure. Biting lips indicates pressure, while tilting your head to the side demonstrates submission and/or thoughtfulness. On a closer level, dilated eyes show interest and curiosity.[4]

For most of us, the signs are obvious. We get most of our information about the world through our eyes and so are constantly "reading" the appearance of the people around us. The secret for a successful speaker involves being aware of the messages that listeners are sending subliminally. At my first meeting as executive director, for example, some staffers stood erect, with arms folded across their chests. That's clearly a defensive, defiant gesture. People leaning forward were indicating interest.

I always try to be aware of the basic body signals of others. People perform them unconsciously, giving a careful observer hints into their inner thoughts. Everything matters: where people sit in relation to one another; what they sit on; and how they are arranged with respect to the furniture and setting. This is true for a large gathering or a private meeting.

As a result, I arranged the chairs in my office for the one-on-one sessions so that the employee did not sit directly across from me with my desk separating us. That positioning can seem confrontational or intimidating. Instead, I moved the chair to the side of the desk. That way, the employee was almost on a level with me. The chair also was not placed against the desk, but a few inches back. That provided some private space for the employee. Too close, and a person feels crowded; too far away, and it's much harder to create feelings of trust.

I also leaned back and relaxed as I spoke with employees. Each person who came to my office for a meeting was offered a piece of candy. My opening was pleasant: a cheery welcome, a handshake. I did everything I could to make the employee feel comfortable despite being called into the office the way a student may be hauled into a principal's office at school. We all dreaded that, even if we hadn't done anything wrong. A big smile and candy helped allay fears.

I knew each staffer would initially feel uncomfortable, so I tried to help them relax. I answered questions honestly and listened to them. I did care what they were thinking, but they could know that only if I focused on them while they talked. If I fiddled with a pen or checked out paperwork, they could get the message that I did not care. Instead, each employee got my undivided attention.

Such efforts really paid off. The agency quickly recovered its balance. We found some solid new employees to replace those who left.

But part of that success was also due to oral communication.

Oral: Choose Your Words Wisely

Just as how I appeared to the employees was important, so was what I said. That includes everything from tone to word choice.

I began my initial meeting at EDCSPIN (just as I've begun these types of meetings ever since) by analyzing my audience. I recognized that I would be talking to an edu-cated group of employees: social workers, all of whom had college degrees. Many came from highly rated universities. In some ways these meetings were akin to my first few days at Lincoln University, where I was acutely aware of how bet-ter prepared the other students were. In this case, however, I was older and more experienced, and I held a law degree from a fine university. As a result, I could talk to employees on their level.

That was very important. We've all heard people who use big words and try to impress listeners with their vocabulary. I wasn't trying to wow anyone. I just wanted to be sure to communicate my intentions.

As with all presentations, I started with the basic question: What did my audience need to know? Staffers at EDCSPIN needed to be aware that there had been a change in leadership, but that their income and careers were not affected. People are always interested in the impact of change on their lives. They wanted to know what would happen next; I told them. They wanted their questions answered; I did that too. I spoke clearly, but I did not raise my voice, which would have implied that I was dictating to them. I also didn't whisper, which could denote fear. After all, we were in a large room, and I needed the people in the back to hear what I said and not have to ask someone nearby for a translation.

I tried to be natural; I was talking with my colleagues, not lecturing. As in all speeches, I stressed the key points, which meant reminding everyone at the conclusion about what was going to be the next step—individual meetings.

I also tried to look at everyone, but not for a long time at any single person. People can get intimidated if a speaker focuses on them. However, by looking around the room, I included everyone in the process.

My tone of voice was also a very deliberate choice. It's possible to say the same thing with inflections that change the meaning. Think of the first words I said: "Some of you know me. For the rest, let me introduce myself. More than a decade ago, I helped start this agency. Some of you know I have been on the board of directors. As of today, I am your chief executive officer."

If I had said those first words in a haughty manner, I would have turned off the staff. If I had said them in a defiant way, I could have set up a confrontation. Instead, I was conversational. I established my credentials as one of the agency's founders and then emphasized the main point. I emphasized my new status by smiling. The silent message enhanced the spoken one.

I made sure the message was on target, clear, and brief. We've all heard people talk too long, like ministers at church who forget to end their sermon.

None of this happened by accident. I had to think about my message. When I first began working, I didn't have these skills. Today I am confident in my ability to speak before any group. That confidence came from practice, teaching as an adjunct professor at Baruch College, and lecturing on behalf of the American Association on Intellectual and Developmental Disabilities, along with speaking to various audiences throughout the region. Control of one's tone is like any other skill; it improves with practice.

Written: Redraft the Script

The oral presentation went well, but it had to be reinforced. That's where writing came in. Written communication allowed me to continue the effort to gain the staff's support even when I could not be present.

Even the sign posted for the first meeting was consciously part of that effort. It was typed and printed. It looked professional. It had only the necessary words: "Staff Meeting 8:45 a.m. Tuesday." That was all.

The email to the staff was equally brief and to the point: "Please contact me to set up a meeting to discuss how we can work together to continue the work of EDCSPIN."

Nothing in the notes was threatening. At the same time, the wording clearly stated the objective of the meeting.

Good written communication is vital. For starters, everything written can potentially become a legal document. With written communication, we can trace services given to a client and the progress of a particular case. Such records are both permanent and proof of our efforts that can be provided to regulatory agencies and funding bodies.

At the same time, written communication must be clear or it can create confusion. This is especially true since there's no chance for immediate feedback. I could tell how people felt during my nonverbal and oral communication from their reactions during my brief orientation and in our private sessions, but I didn't see how people reacted to their email.

Written communication does, however, allow for a consistent message. That's evident from the EDCSPIN website, which includes pictures of families with the repeated message that all of us are important and everyone has to work together. The images are pleasant, the colors pastel. The pages exude a sense of peace and enjoyment. Our website also highlights the agency's values: integrity, respect, opportunity, accountability, and togetherness.

Our main message is the focus on togetherness. That idea is emphasized in the "About Us" section: "We consider it a privilege to serve our communities and we are proud of how much has been accomplished in our first two decades. The difference we have made in so many lives could only have been accomplished through the extraordinary effort of a dedicated staff working together."

The concept is also featured in my biography on the website: "Charles Montorio-Archer firmly believes that 'Everybody is required for Everything!' and he's more than willing to do his part."

If I said that repeatedly, everyone would be bored. However, the idea can be presented in many ways in writing, providing a clear image of what the agency thinks is important. The same theme is picked up on EverybodyPaddles.com, which has a quote from me on the front page: "Everybody paddles . . . at the same time, in the same direction, toward the same goal."

Written communication has two key components: grammar and clarity. The writing must be grammatically correct. I like to think of grammar as a code that everyone knows and follows. Nothing can cause confusion faster than changing the code. It makes things very difficult to understand.

Jesus ran into the problem of changing the code with his parables. Not everyone could understand because he was presenting information in an unfamiliar way. The meanings became clear only after much study, explanation, and understanding.

The same cannot be said, however, for written communication replete with major grammatical or spelling errors. Instead, the reader gets an unwritten message that the writer was careless, uninterested, and possibly illiterate. Few of us will glean anything useful from that kind of writing, nor will we respect the person who produced it.

At the same time, word choice and tone must be appropriate for the audience. Just as with an oral presentation, written communication must be directed at and appropriate for the intended audience.

Business leaders all recognize this. Gilbert Amelio, former president and CEO of National Semiconductor Corporation, spoke for many executives when he said: "Developing excellent communication skills is absolutely essential to effective leadership. The leader must be able to share knowledge and ideas to transmit a sense of urgency and enthusiasm to others. If a leader can't get a message across clearly and motivate others to act on it, then having a message doesn't even matter."[5]

Scott Barkin, a colleague, friend, and executive director at Block Institute, also spoke about the need for united action: "Our job is to get everyone to row in the same direction."

I couldn't have said it better.

◆ ◆ ◆

Christian A. Paul, a banking executive from Saint Lucia, has Caribbean-wide leadership experience. In his "Perspective" essay, he contributes his thoughts on that leadership and on the value of cooperation. As you will see, he is a skilled practitioner of the art of effective leadership communication.

PERSPECTIVE: EQUIP THEM WITH PADDLES

Christian A. Paul, Sales and Business Development,
Insurance Corporation of Barbados (ICBL)

In December 1997 I was appointed country manager of the Anguilla branch of an international bank. I was hired by the bank's regional director at its regional head office in Barbados, where I worked at the time. I felt like I was eight feet tall. After all, I was thirty-two years old, one of the younger managers to hold such a position. Yes, I felt very proud, and I felt that I deserved it because of my experience and also because I put everything I had into my work.

So, one month later, I was on a flight to Anguilla, ready to change the world! But as I arrived at my new work location, I was unprepared for what I saw. The building looked dilapidated, with moss growing on its faded walls. Were it not for the bank's unmistakable logo on the walls, I would have thought that the taxi had taken me to the wrong place. Nevertheless, I settled in at my hotel with eager anticipation. After all, as my uncle Roger would always say, "A coat of paint can hide a multitude of sins," and surely that's all it would take to get the place looking spick-and-span—or so I thought.

The next morning, all decked out and spiffy, I arrived at the bank. If I wasn't prepared for the state of the building the day before, I would never have been prepared by what I found inside: broken tiles, dated countertops, shabby furniture, and old boxes. The place resembled an old warehouse, and the staff didn't present much better in terms of demeanor.

Who could blame them? They had taken on the character of their surroundings. In short, the ship of my career was heading toward an iceberg, and it was going to be difficult to negotiate a safe course. By this time, my exaggerated sense of stature had quickly returned to my normal 5 feet 9 inches, and my shoulders slumped under the weight of the dreary surroundings.

In the weeks that followed, I learned of the promises by two previous managers to repair the building. This explained why the staff had laughed when, at my first meeting, I said I was going to effect renovations to the building. The employees there were not even in the same boat, much less having paddles.

I decided right there and then that if I was going to have any chance of leading this business with this team, I needed to communicate that change was possible by tackling the physical environment. I reasoned that the condition of the building impacted not only staff morale but also performance.

Armed with little more than instinct and my life experiences thus far, I went about making plans and soliciting assistance from the head office. The original budgets for the renovations took account only of the customer areas, because the staff areas were in good condition at the time. However, the eight years that had elapsed since then had taken a toll on these areas as well. I took a stance: We either renovated everywhere or nowhere. That became my singular focus: First fix the boat that was leaking, and then get the staff on board.

My gamble paid off, and we got things going. We

renovated the building, changed furniture, and got staff new uniforms. The boat had been fixed, and it was time to start the journey of repositioning the business, but I still needed people on board to help me get where I wanted to go.

I began by refocusing on earlier initiatives to create a sustained sales and customer service culture. Refurbishing the premises and physical amenities had given us a start, and the staff became gradually more receptive to the various strategies and initiatives to regain a foothold in the market and start growing the business. They began to want to go on the journey, and as we painted a picture of what success would look like, they began to see our destination more clearly. The other, equally important catalyst was reassuring them that we would be doing this together. I had built a massive amount of credibility by delivering on the promise I made when I first arrived, and that credibility earned me the right to ask them to journey with me.

This time I set about creating a high-energy environment. Businesses on the island engaged one another in friendly competition in different sporting disciplines, and we participated in those games. I also included all staff (from messenger to senior supervisor—all seventeen of them) at the annual cocktail party to welcome a visiting director of the bank. In the past, only supervisors were invited, but my thinking was that there were not many staff at the branch and the added cost would therefore not be significant. Also, I needed the staff present to help introduce me to customers in attendance with whom they interacted every day. In turn, that act communicated a certain impression to customers, many of whom commented on it at the cocktail party and during the weeks that followed. So, people on the outside, too, were starting to notice a difference!

We built more momentum by getting involved in community events. This island was known for its boat-racing tradition in which wooden canoes and schooners sailed the surrounding waters, challenging one another for bragging rights in fierce but friendly competition. The corporate community was always a part of this cultural activity—though my bank had never been. This, then, was an opportunity to expose the brand further, and we sponsored one of the boats by paying for a large sail and T-shirts for the crew and supporters, including our staff. Many people singled us out for praise for finally getting involved in this important aspect of the island's culture. While I felt vindicated by seeing the impact on the community at large, I was even more pleased at the pride the staff exhibited at being part of a company that supported such an event.

This positive energy was then channeled into sales activities by staff who were now believers and to a community that had noticed the change and was now receptive to our brand. Staff members were firmly in the boat, believing in the journey and starting to paddle toward our destination. We did more community outreach, and because of customer visits at which staff were more buoyant, the quality of the in-branch customer experience soared.

We ran into some turbulent waters because of inexperience among the staff, but with the assistance of the head office and after bringing in some experienced staff members from the region, the blend of youth and experience made for good team dynamics. By the second year of my tenure in Anguilla, we led the regional country branches, having the highest percentage of loan sales results against target.

Though I was transferred via promotion after my third year in Anguilla, and despite the fact that since that time I have had the opportunity to lead many teams around the region in different areas of banking, I can honestly say that my first two years as manager in Anguilla were my most rewarding assignment. Not only was it my first managerial appointment, it was also important because my conviction in my beliefs and my leadership were vindicated.

As a leader, your role is to open doors, build bridges, and remove barriers. You must teach and coach; you must be firm but fair; you must create the team and make that team the center and the focus. In the end, leadership is about getting employees into the boat and giving them what they need to start paddling.

PERSPECTIVE: COLLABORATION THROUGH COMMUNICATION

Kelcey Liverpool, Founder and Executive Director, Kids Rank

I met Charles in October 2013 when he was matched as my mentor during the *Inc.* Magazine 5000 Conference focused on the country's fastest growing entrepreneurial companies. My nonprofit was just under two years old, and I was chosen as a participant for the military track recognizing promising business ventures from across the country. From the start, Charles and I had a connection that felt like we had known each other for years—a level of comfort where he was, and still is, able to give me constructive feedback and push me further as a leader than I would ever do on my own. He forces me to recognize my strength and great potential and to step forward in a way that is authentic to who I am. Over the last eight years I can say that I have grown, and Charles continues to inspire me to think bigger. I like to take ideas and bring solutions that help build communities. I have a passion for designing programs and initiatives that create change. My background includes work within the arts, banking, and nonprofit sectors with the common thread of relationship building and design. I believe, when working in a human service industry, that nothing meaningful is built alone, as the strengths and voices from many perspectives are required to adequately address the needs of others. This is how I approach work and own my role as a creative leader.

Most notably, I am the founder and executive director of Kids Rank, established in 2012 as a nonprofit organization designed specifically to support the social and emotional well-being of military and veteran children. Through the formation of local clubs, called Prides, Kids Rank engages children in hands-on skill-building projects and volunteer opportunities designed to encourage resilience through our core pillars of CONNECT, LEAD, and SERVE. This niche population is not generally thought of when people discuss our military service members. Military-connected youth are found in every zip code across the United States and in many countries around the world. Oftentimes policy and initiative focus take shape around the service person or the spouse, but the perspective and impact of the military child is largely missing. Military families are immersed in our civilian communities, yet there is a large disconnect between the communities and families. Roughly 70 percent of military families do not live on a base, and approximately 80 percent of the children attend public school. An active-duty child averages six to eight schools within their K–12 education career and moves roughly every two to three years.

I have lived this life, as I was a navy spouse for over seventeen years, moving with my family a total of nine times and volunteering in several roles at various military installation agencies. I have two military children of my own, now seventeen and nineteen, who made all those moves, including one of which was overseas to Japan. With each move, my girls had to change schools, meet new friends, and leave behind connections and relationships that they had grown to rely on. Witnessing these transitions, not only for my own children but also the other children in our community, revealed a gap in services available to them. Research around the impact of military life on the children of those who serve is only about twenty years old despite the armed services being in existence 245 years. Only more recently have researchers and organizations begun to address the unique challenges faced by this population and the potential long-term impact. However, the scope in services to date has consisted mainly of organizations that specialize in advocacy that addresses only some of the many challenges, particularly within the education system. Other services provide episodic workshops or camps around specific topic areas, but none address the need for ongoing continuous programming to build a sense of belonging from a holistic perspective. One of the biggest challenges for children who experience so much transition is their disconnection from the communities they are currently calling home. I understand firsthand the challenges children and families of service members face, and I feel it is important to focus on the whole child, recognizing both their strengths and challenges. In addition to peer-to-peer connections, which give them a space to share their excitement, fears, and feelings in a safe environment, we must also have a vetted network of care educated in military culture.

Over the past nine years, under my leadership and management of effective partnerships, Kids Rank has grown as a trusted organization, providing consistent quality programming in the Illinois military and veteran community. Thanks to mentorship early on, I learned the beauty of focusing our efforts to stay mission focused, do what we do really well, and partner with others who are experts in their fields to elevate achievement of our goals. As a result, I have successfully built strong relationships and partnered with several organizations, such as the Sesame Workshop, National Veterans Art Museum, USO Illinois, the Red Cross, the Military Child Education Coalition, and others in an effort to further the Kids Rank mission and awareness of supporting the needs of military-connected children. I look at relationship building as a long game that has the potential of getting stronger over time—meeting, getting to know each other, finding common goals, and working together in a way that showcases the value added by each party.

In October 2020, we launched a series called Foundations: A Conversation on Military Youth Mental Health and Well-Being. Even before the global pandemic, many military youths found themselves in situations that caused feelings of isolation, anxiety, and many other factors that created added stress to their mental health and well-being. I wanted to be a part of a system that is proactive in our offering of support in an effort to mitigate the potential negative impact that growing up in a military family can present. Through Foundations, as part of monthly hour-long sessions on different topic areas, we get to explore the landscape of who and what services are available for our military children in providing reliable resources. In addition, because of the participation of families and providers, we are continuing to learn where there are gaps in services. The collaborative process of work that I developed in the years prior to the Foundations Conversations has now begun to click together to form a beautiful tapestry of collective support.

Currently, my board and a group of dedicated stakeholders are engaged in a strategic planning process to discuss a road map for national expansion for Kids Rank. A key component of this plan will be mapped out from our collaborative network of school districts, military installations, community organizations, and funding partners to create a blueprint strengthening our ability to provide the best care for our military youth as we continue to grow. Most collaboration requires leadership, although the form of leadership can be social within a decentralized and egalitarian group, which is where I shine. I feel that teams that work collaboratively are able to access greater resources, reach more broadly across their communities, and make deeper impact often while best utilizing the finite funding pools available. Collaboration is a core value for me, both personally and professionally, and I believe that it has proven to be my biggest source of inspiration and success.

PERSPECTIVE: COMMUNICATING THROUGH CRISIS

Bela Moté, CEO, Carole Robertson Center for Learning

In June 2018, I became CEO of the Carole Robertson Center for Learning. Our Center is one of the largest early childhood and youth development nonprofit organizations in Chicago, serving more than one thousand children and their families every day, with a significant presence on the city's West Side.

I was the fourth CEO—and the first outside CEO—since the organization's founding in 1976. The community areas we serve have undergone increasing population stabilization and revitalization since the turn of the century but still face immense economic challenges and barriers to access. And all too often, their trust has been eroded by outsiders parachuting in without authentic or lasting engagement. Coming in as an outsider, I needed to demonstrate my willingness to serve as a true, long-term partner while maintaining and advancing the Center's standing as a trusted resource.

Early on in my tenure, Chicago was in turmoil, gripped by coverage of the trial of former Chicago police officer Jason Van Dyke, who was ultimately convicted for the 2014 murder of Laquan McDonald. Of course, this same pain and trauma has manifested itself in many other instances of police brutality and racial

injustice in the times before and since Laquan McDonald's death. This deeply painful and sensitive context led
me on my own journey of reflection as I grappled with
what it meant to be a person of Indian descent leading
an organization that primarily serves Black and Latinx
families. I could never deliberately diminish or trivialize
the lived experience of others, nor could I put my own
experiences on a shelf. As a first-generation American
who immigrated to the United States at a young age
and grew up in Chicago, I sought to strike an authentic balance between recognizing common ground and
connection on an individual level without seeking to
equate my experiences with those of others.

I started by making a concerted effort to show up
for community conversations as a listener and learner
first. It was important for me to communicate to all of
the Center's stakeholders—including our families, our
neighborhoods, and our staff—that I was approaching
my role with humility, conviction, and care, and with an
appreciation of what was at stake. I engaged with other
nonprofit human service organizations and schools serving the neighborhoods where the Center has a strong
presence, and I also started to identify the proverbial
tables that existed that our organization should have a
seat at; I joined several locally based committees and
coalitions and encouraged my staff to do the same. This

type of engagement demonstrates that the organization is invested in uplifting the communities we serve, even beyond the boundaries of our discrete programs. Encouraging this same approach by my staff was a recognition that being an ally and partner doesn't just live with me.

Meanwhile, on an organizational level, some of my key departmental leadership positions were vacant, and others turned over as part of the transition. I learned the nuts and bolts of the organization by filling in as the department manager in every single department over the course of my first year. For example, I had no chief financial officer; thus, I learned the budget, the bills paid, and the contract and compliance issues. As challenging as that time was, I would do it all over again because it allowed me to learn the underbelly of the organization and to understand how our people think, work, and communicate.

My first two years as CEO were a boot camp in the importance of leadership communication. This was especially true given the nature of our work and employee base, which is spread across multiple locations and includes both administrative and frontline (teaching, family support, mental health) staff. As CEO, my daily interactions with broad swaths of staff members can be minimal at times, which makes keeping the lines of communication open all the more important.

Transparency and authenticity are key, especially in periods of major change like those that come with new leadership, because they can help alleviate fear and uncertainty. I communicated with staff members often via written updates that I penned personally. My philosophy is that it's better for the staff to hear directly from me, even if the honest answer is "I don't know," than for them to assume or guess at something bigger that no one is sharing with them. I also practiced a true open-door policy and welcomed staff to contact me directly. And I visited the early childhood and youth development programs in our two flagship buildings, along with spending time at our offsite programs, including home visiting services. I met regularly with teachers and family support staff to hear straight from them about the opportunities and challenges in their work.

I will never ask a staff person to do a task that I wouldn't do myself, and that is another principle I communicated through my actions: helping soothe a crying child in a program, cleaning and organizing our office space, or simply being available as a listening ear and partner in finding solutions to difficult problems. As a result of this work, my staff could see me as an accessible, approachable CEO, in part because they actually saw me in our shared spaces. On a material level, I was able to elevate base salaries by $7,000 on average, further demonstrating the staff's enormous value to our mission. I believe that these efforts reaped enormous benefits for me and our Center, and our turnover rate decreased after my first year as CEO.

Every night, I go to bed asking myself, "Did I do all I could today to do right by our staff, children, and families?" The answer is what grounds me in the mission of the Carole Robertson Center. In March 2020, as we were plunged into a global pandemic, that question would be more important than ever before. The Carole Robertson Center responded to the pandemic in creative and nimble ways to ensure that we continued to meet the needs of our communities. This included hosting distributions for essential goods like diapers, formula, and food, and opening our doors to Chicago Public Schools students in need of a safe and structured space for e-learning.[6]

The tenets of servant leadership have always been embedded in my work, but their importance was highlighted during these tumultuous times. From the onset of the pandemic, I and my executive leadership team prioritized working alongside frontline staff in carrying out our emergency response work. A typical day for me early in the pandemic might have included virtual meetings with city and state leaders to advocate for continued funding, followed by a trip to one of our centers to assemble learning packets and hand out diapers to families. These actions communicated to our staff how important their work was and that, through thick and thin, the organization's leaders would be right beside them.

It was important to me to recognize the trauma that our staff members were undergoing through this pandemic as well. To navigate the uncertainty and keep staff members connected, I instituted two new mechanisms for staff-wide communication and connection at the start of the pandemic: town halls and mindfulness sessions.

The town hall sessions needed to address two important realities. First, people needed to be heard. Second, it was going to take all of us, working toward the same goals, to navigate the ever-changing landscape that COVID created. We needed a way to stay connected and communicate with one another, and we also needed a platform where we could problem-solve and innovate in real time. All town halls were conducted via video conference, but we made an intentional decision to structure these as open meetings rather than webinars in presentation mode. This meant that staff members could see one another. It also meant that no one was muted. These seemingly small decision points had a big effect. As one staff member noted, "We were treated equally. We were asked what we thought and what we were comfortable with. And the leadership team listened."

The same week that the pandemic shutdown began, we also instituted weekly mindfulness sessions for staff, facilitated by the Center's senior manager of mental health. These thirty-minute meetings were an opportunity for staff to connect with one another and focus on themselves. The time was protected—we did not schedule other internal meetings during these appointments—in order to demonstrate that this was a priority for the organization. Despite all the chaos, we found a way to come together as a staff and build our collective resiliency.

As the pandemic raged on, our nation also faced a renewed reckoning with racial injustice, sparked in large part by the murder of George Floyd in May 2020. I convened an all-staff conversation where staff could come together, share their experiences, and engage in self-reflection in a supportive and honest atmosphere. I could have gone down the roster of staff members and asked another to facilitate, but I recognized that everyone was experiencing their own trauma caused by systemic racial oppression. I also ruled out hiring an outside consultant for this purpose. How could I bring someone in who didn't know us and expect staff members to open up about the things they were processing?

I knew that if I passed the ball, I wasn't doing all that I could do as the leader of this organization. It was clear we needed to come together and be together, to serve our children and families. I knew I couldn't solve every pain created by systemic racism and inequity, but what I could do was express my commitment to not repeating those mistakes at the Carole Robertson Center. Essentially, I could listen. So I did.

The Carole Robertson Center was the one of the first of Chicago's early childhood and youth development programs to reopen after Illinois lifted its shutdown order. This is a testament to the resiliency and capabilities of our staff. Our shared experiences through the pandemic have been unprecedented in nearly every way, but I believe that our transparent, honest, and authentic communications as a staff during this time have enabled the organization to thrive and continue to serve as a vital resource to our communities.

Our people are the heartbeat of the Carole Robertson Center, our mission in motion. Every single piece of the organization—every staff person—must work together to support this, paddling together to ensure that we never lose sight of our North Star: the children we have the opportunity to serve in our programs.

PERSPECTIVE: COMMUNICATION, COMMUNITY, AND ENGAGEMENT

Nicole Robinson, Chief Partnership and Programs Officer,
Greater Chicago Food Depository

The concept of "Everybody Paddles" is powerful in its simplicity, impact, and unifying ability to connect people behind a collective vision. As a nonprofit human services executive, I am drawn to concepts that are grounded in unleashing the potential of people across community, government, and business to advance a shared, more equitable humanity. In my role as chief partnerships and programs officer at the Greater Chicago Food Depository, I have the privilege to work alongside a Chicagoland community committed to ensuring families have access to nutritious food through neighborhood food pantries, government nutrition assistance programs, and economic opportunities.

Although this is my profession, my interest is deeply personal, informed by my early life growing up on Chicago's South Side. Raised by a single mother, along with support from my grandmother and brother, I grew up in a warm and loving household but one burdened by economic stress, the perceived shame of receiving food stamps and reliance on the public health system. I am also a product of public schools, explorer of the world through public libraries, youth camp participant at city public parks, and the beneficiary of government and nonprofit programs. These experiences and investments unleashed my potential and shaped who I am as a leader today.

What has always struck me about the early years of my life is that my family and others of similar circumstances regularly navigated systems and programs to meet basic needs—food, shelter, education, and healthcare. Our society celebrates the success of a few without dealing with the reality that too many of our systems and programs have unwarranted complexity and do not work for everyone. In Chicago this is further complicated by our deep divisions, as reflected through racial segregation, multigenerational poverty, unaddressed trauma, as well as economic and political inequity.

As I reflect Everybody Paddles, I believe it is the responsibility of leaders to ensure everyone in the boat feels a sense of belonging, that everyone has a highly functioning paddle, and that they are equipped with the training, coaching, and experiences needed to be successful. I believe Everybody Paddles can be a catalyst for transformational change and movement building for people within our institutions and most importantly for the people we serve.

My personal commitment to ensuring my team

members reach their full potential runs deep. During my early tenure at the Greater Chicago Food Depository, I inherited a team that was slightly demoralized, disempowered, and not reflective of the communities we serve, but at the same time, it was a smart, talented, and mission-driven team. As a new leader to the team, I wanted to accomplish two things right away. First, I wanted to understand how team members understand their goals and responsibilities as well as how they connected those goals to others across the organization. Second, I wanted to understand who they are as people and who they aspired to be either inside the organization or outside the organization. Our biggest chance of accomplishing anything transformational or radical inside our organizations and communities is rooted in our ability to invest in the professional and personal growth of people.

I tapped into my previous experiences to offer my team a process to ensure every person on the team had a growth and development plan. Formalized development planning processes ensure that every employee has an opportunity to reflect on their strengths, opportunities for improvements, and overall aspirations. I was able to quickly understand who the self-identified project management whizzes were, the research mavens, the powerhouse presenters, and the food insecurity policy technical experts. At the same time, I learned who struggled to navigate the organization, felt overlooked, sensed they were underutilized, operated in fear, and were just plain bored.

The plan itself focused on actions each person could take to strengthen leadership competencies or build brand-new skills. I hold on to the belief that the experiences of working on projects drives 70 percent of our learning, while 20 percent is gained from coaching/feedback from colleagues, and 10 percent is through training courses. I recall during those first development planning meetings, I had at least three employees who, after asking them to reflect on their strengths and their aspirations, were all overcome with a wave of emotion that evoked tears. In all cases, some past traumatic stifling work experiences shaped their reaction, but each employee's tears were ones of relief and hope that they had permission to think about how they could excel in the moment, while building a professional tool kit for their future.

More so than any institutions, I believe that nonprofit and government institutions have a responsibility to help individuals, communities, and the broader society reach their full potential. One of the biggest barriers toward that goal is inequity, and unfortunately it is the barrier that brings us the most discomfort. Whether you are a member of the White majority or a Black Indigenous Person of Color (BIPOC) we all have been institutionalized to be silent on matters of race, which has resulted in leaving a whole group of people behind— economically, socially, and politically. A global public health economic and food security pandemic disproportionately impacted Black and Brown communities. This combined with an incomprehensible number of Black deaths to police brutality drove a reckoning on structural racism that awakened the world to speak up and speak out.

My leadership journey to bring equity to the Greater Chicago Food Depository as an institution began several years before the pandemic. As I began to review food insecurity rates by geography and race, it became very apparent that 90 percent of clients who visited a food pantry identify as a race or ethnicity other than White. The top ten neighborhoods with the highest rates of poverty, unemployment, chronic health conditions, lowest life expectancy, and the highest rates of returning citizens are the Black and Brown communities disproportionately impacted by food insecurity. Rates of food insecurity rates near 30–40 percent in Black and Brown communities and prepandemic employment rates were already double digit. Although the data was clear, there was initially internal resistance to discuss the role racism plays in why people are food insecure and to openly discuss how to account for race in our vision, mission, and strategies. As a Black woman leader who has dealt with challenges of racism throughout my life and intuitively understands inequity, I honestly was not skilled at helping my White colleagues understand racial inequity and how they could be antiracist in our mission.

However, I started with my boss, the CEO and executive director, who would ultimately become my biggest and most impactful ally in this journey. After experiencing a transformational racial equity training session produced by Race Forward, one of the nation's leaders in the racial justice movement, I walked into the CEO's office and plainly said, "We will not fulfill our mission if we do not embed racial equity into our work. Black and Brown people will continue to be food insecure." This initial conversation was the catalyst that would result in the Food Depository Governance Board and leadership team making a commitment to racial equity. Examples of this commitment included the training of over two hundred employees, establishment of a supplier diversity spending strategy and targets (quote numbers), and hiring people of color while being race explicit in our communication and programmatic strategies. The training helped us adopt a common understanding.

However, embracing racial equity requires organizational transformation. Similar to other leadership values and competencies e.g., dealing with ambiguity, presentation skills—you must flex it like a muscle and apply the concepts in everyday program development and policy making to actually put the knowledge to good use.

Although these early efforts did cover the full dimensions of equity, diversity, and inclusion—by beginning with racial equity, we tackled the most challenging, uncomfortable, and institutionalized aspects of the work that unknowingly prepared us for the COVID-19 pandemic that would brutally bring sickness, trauma, and death to Black and Brown communities already burdened by food insecurity.

During the height of the pandemic, I ensured the Food Depository was committed to ensuring all food pantries could remain open and operational during a time where we saw a 150 percent increase in demand for food assistance. Immediately, our research & evaluation manager helped me see that not every Chicago neighborhood had adequate food access to meet the new demand. This data inspired me to consider how we could close this gap by empowering Black and Latino faith, organizers, and community-based groups to lead their own pop-up food distributions. The concept was simple. The Food Depository would provide the food, training, and cash grants. The organizers, faith institutions, and community organizations would mobilize people to stand shoulder to shoulder together in food distribution, while making it easy for neighbors who may have never visited a pantry to feel comfortable, to feel some relief. We launched this in May of 2020 with seven organizations, and I asked each group to make a commitment to weekly food distributions over six weeks. Nearly every partner distributed food through Thanksgiving 2020, well beyond their commitment, but it was a response to the need.

While the pop-up food distributions were underway, the demand for food in Black and Latino communities remained at record levels. The fragility of the entire food system was tested from retail grocery stores to food pantries—and we were all reminded that securing nutritious food for Black and Latino families is inequitable in access and experience. It is unjust! This is exacerbated by the fact that many food pantries are under-resourced. Seventy percent of the Food Depository community partners have a budget of $50,000 or less, and 34 percent have zero to five staff members, which is why many food pantries are operated by volunteers.

For me, the path to building a stronger, more resilient emergency food system is one that invests in the food access programs that are designed by, informed by, and led by community members. It is a path that shares power. To bring this path to life, in February 2021 we invested $2.6MM in twenty-six organizations located in Black and Latino communities—four of which would open new pantries based on community vision. Twenty-two organizations received funds to expand their operations and provide better service. It is inspiring to witness the creative genius of the new partners; before the pandemic they would have never imagined opening a food pantry. As social justice institutions, they are acutely aware of the inequities; that public policies are needed to reduce the wealth divide; and to expand employment opportunities necessary to make food pantries obsolete. However, they do this work now to support what some experts say will be a decade-long economic recovery.

These investments are merely the first step. They have helped catalyze a movement that seeks to reduce the inequities in the food system. The power of Everybody Paddles is that as leaders, policymakers, parishioners, advocates, and neighbors we can be responsible to ourselves, each other, our communities, and the institutions we inhabit. As a part of that collective responsibility, we must stand together in solidarity to solve some of Chicago's toughest social, economic, and political challenges. As civic leaders we must create compassionate space to hear each other and see each other—even when we do not agree. Dr. Martin Luther King Jr. expressed it best when he said, "We are tied together in a single garment of destiny, caught in an inescapable network of mutuality. I can never be what I ought to be until you are what you ought to be. And you can never be what you ought to be, until I am what I ought to be." Through our investments in people, both those inside our organization and the community members we work alongside, we are closer to creating a more just, a more equitable society.

Principle Five

PROBLEM SOLVING, COURSE CORRECTION

~~~

Every day I'm in the office, employees come in to talk to me. My door is always open, and I welcome their visits. Naturally, they are not dropping by to chat; they know I am busy. They have a chain of command and use it. Still, on occasion, some issue arises, and they need to speak to me. In doing so, they are verifying that I am part of their team. They instinctively understand that everything they do affects me, and vice versa.

But that's not how things started out. We may have been in the same boat and headed in the same direction, but not everyone was paddling the same way. Even after our first big meeting and after the smaller one-on-one sessions with each employee, I could see that they were still divided into cliques or had adopted a "we-they" attitude. The mood throughout the agency was corrosive. Many were selfish, having a "me-first" mentality. Others disliked me because I was in the director's office and their former leader wasn't.

That last part was understandable. Some of my new staff members were naturally wary of change, as most people are. Others were concerned that I would not keep my promise to maintain jobs. They felt that the agency's troubles could cause it to fold, taking their positions with it. Others were sure that nothing would be different and rejected anything I said. Only a few people at first were willing to give me a chance.

My challenge, now that I was the chief executive officer, was to change that attitude and create a team. It's the same daunting task that faces any new leader. I was unknown to them; there was no reason for them to embrace me immediately. Their hesitancy was compounded by the reality that I headed a $10-million-a-year agency with dozens of employees. I was responsible not just to them but also to the hundreds of disabled clients who counted on EDCSPIN for services.

Develop Change Agents

Change came slowly. The truth is that old cultures tend to cling with all the tenacity of Velcro. They refuse to disappear. People develop habits based on an existing culture and then conform their activities to it. I was bringing in entirely new concepts: an openness that the staff immediately distrusted because it was so counter to the approach of the previous

administration; an emphasis on honesty, which was necessary after problems with the former director; and fairness in
hiring and in recognition. That was a lot for anyone to absorb.

All of my subliminal messages and email to employees
described earlier could not weld them into a team. I had to
start by recognizing the basic reality that my employees came
to the agency first to get a job and second because they enjoy
helping people. Everything else about them was different, from
appearance and background to outside activities and family. They represented varied interests, different ideas. Some
would never take the initiative; others would, even if it meant
overriding a basic rule. Most, like the majority of employees
everywhere, went along with the flow to avoid problems.

My first step was to encourage everyone to focus on the
same goal. That divorced the staff from concentrating on personnel changes and policy differences to think about what
we all had in common. We were all working hard to provide
services to "individuals with developmental disabilities and/
or mental retardation" to give them "the opportunity to learn
skills needed to reach their highest level of independence
all while insuring they experience the same privileges and
opportunities enjoyed by all members of our society," as our
website states.

That approach then fueled my conversations with my colleagues. I asked each person who met with me the same basic
questions: What can we do better? What suggestions can you

recommend? How can we resolve problems? That opened the door to constructive criticism and meaningful feedback. Not everyone was willing to speak up, but a handful were willing to trust me and described the working conditions they wanted improved. Several had excellent ideas for implementing the necessary kinds of changes. I wrote them down and, one by one, implemented those that would work. I also credited the employee who proposed the given change.

That was an essential step in the welding process. Many employees simply felt that their voices were not being heard. Previously, they saw how cronies were rewarded while those actually doing the work were shunted aside. Now they saw how I was trying to change the culture within the agency. They were eager to join me. They became my first change agents.

As one person and then the next began to alter attitudes, others followed. I could almost feel the atmosphere lighten. When I first came into the building, employees would glance at me with sullen looks, as if expecting me to morph into some kind of sinister taskmaster. Often, work simply stopped. Staffers waited for me to disappear into my office, as if they had been caught doing something wrong. It was eerie and disheartening to see how employees reacted to my presence.

Eventually, when their fears and negative expectations were clearly not being justified and they saw how various directives evened out workloads and rewarded competency, they began to smile. I could walk in without causing a stir. A couple of people even began to wave or say hello rather than ignoring me. We were becoming a team.

Be Consistent

To maintain the progress, I also realized that the message had to be consistent. It would not help to say one thing and do another. For example, I recall when Ford Motor Company began to advertise in the early 1980s that "Quality is Job 1." The campaign came in response to inroads made by the Japanese automakers into the American automobile market. Unfortunately, Ford merely made claims; the actual manufacture of cars did not catch up to the verbiage. So, buyers began to associate Ford with poorly made cars. That has changed only recently, when the company hype finally began to be matched by quality cars. Today, Ford consistently scores well in quality rankings.

I did not want to be in the position of talking the talk but not walking the walk. As a result, I did not just talk about providing service to clients; I became certified as a professional in compliance and ethics and in health-care compliance. In addition, I became affiliated with numerous professional associations, which allowed me to lecture and conduct research on a variety of topics important to organizations that provide policy, leadership, and development support as well as community, day, and residential services for the disadvantaged.

In addition, I became a Cuba Research Delegate with the American Association on Intellectual and Developmental Disabilities.

In 2012, I joined the Harvard Kennedy School Driving Government Performance Consortium. I didn't stop there. I began to write articles on a wide range of topics that were published in *Mental Health News*, *City Limits*, and *USA Today*, and on UrbanTimes.com. Copies of my articles were posted in the office. I saw employees read them, obviously happy that their agency and its director were gaining such attention. People want to be proud of where they work, and positive attention boosts that pride.

In addition, I became active in One Hundred Black Men, Inc., of New York City and a volunteer with PENCIL, Inc., which inspires innovation and improves student achievement by partnering business leaders with public schools. My staff saw that I didn't just talk about community service; I did it.

I firmly believe that any leader must set a standard that everyone else can follow. In addition, for a message to work, it must be repeated. Too often, rumors and innuendo have a way of tunneling into any organization and slowly undermining the best intentions. Therefore, it remains important to make sure that the EDCSPIN vision, which is to Enhance the Quality of Life for People with Disabilities, is clearly represented in the values of the organization. To avoid miscommunication, all the material about EDCSPIN (starting with our vision statement) promotes the same concept: Namely, we provide the best service to our one thousand disabled clients, with an emphasis on five key values:

◇ Integrity
◇ Respect
◇ Opportunity
◇ Accountability
◇ Togetherness

Each of these points is continually stressed on our website, in our media releases, and in employee evaluations. They have become an integral aspect of the agency, the lofty goals that each employee tries to ascribe to.

The website further reflects this message with its images of smiling clients and easily accessible information about our mission and values. At the same time, the site includes updates on research in related areas. The pages are bathed in pastel colors that provide warmth and a sense of peace—values that we consistently promote in our day-to-day operations.

The Office: Non-Televised Working Conditions

Aesthetic changes are only a small part of the effort to engage a team in paddling forward together. Employees have to enjoy coming to work, and they have to feel that they are part of an important effort. As a result, I have tried to make EDCSPIN a pleasant place to work, people-wise. And what's good for employees is also good for our clients. No one wants a grumpy social worker showing up at his or her front door or to be greeted by a moody receptionist.

The transformation process involved several steps. First, I eliminated unqualified and underperforming employees who had become far too complacent under the previous administration. I made sure qualified people filled important posts. Staffers were encouraged to continue their education and were then promoted based on their training and abilities, not on their personality or some other arbitrary reason.

Next, knowing that no one is happy working for a supervisor who is inconsiderate or incompetent or incapable, I carefully screened people in leadership roles. Some needed extra training; others—because steps in a process were eliminated or job functions were consolidated or even constant supervision sessions were discontinued—were simply glad to be rid of prior restraints and could function without me constantly looking over their shoulders.

I spent time in my private meetings with employees to identify the quality leaders within the organization. While staffers were often reluctant to discuss the agency as a whole, they didn't hesitate to lambaste department directors and other supervisors they felt were not doing their jobs. That led to more discussions, group meetings, and training sessions. In most cases, the problems were resolved. A few individuals with titles were invited to prepare their resumes to determine their qualifications and experience. I refused to keep anyone on staff at EDCSPIN who channeled the attitudes or behaviors of the unforgiving, dictatorial boss I'd served under as a lobbyist in Albany.

That meant finding replacements. I told you about my Assistant Executive Director of Programs in an earlier chapter, and I was also able to hire several more very competent replacements. I identified others who may not have wanted a title and the responsibility that goes with it, but who exerted leadership through their actions. Many actual leaders do not have a prominent position. They may be quiet, letting their actions speak for them. They may express opinions, but softly. Mostly, though, they guide consensus simply by their presence. I needed them to buy in.

They did, because they could see I was serious. I really listened to them and then fulfilled promises. Nothing is worse than nodding at some suggestion with the hidden intention of ignoring the idea. If an employee recommended a way to improve some procedure, I looked at it very seriously. I did not simply leap in, of course. Everything has to be tested to locate unseen ramifications. Even when an idea was not adopted, employees could see that I had not lightly dismissed it. I also kept notes so I could explain to the person who had proposed the idea why it had not been implemented.

Fortunately, employees were thrilled that I was even

paying attention. They had been ignored for too long. The contrast was between top-down management and the reverse. Too often the American approach has been to let upper management make all the decisions. That does not always work. I'm not suggesting abdicating authority. Rather, I prefer to ensure that everyone affected by any decision has some input into it.

On the other hand, I don't follow the approach pioneered by the Japanese, who hold councils regularly among workers to send proposals to management. Nor do I subscribe to the "management knows best" theory that has dominated American business concepts. My approach is a mix. I am responsible for the final decision, but I seek advice from my staff and welcome their suggestions.

The end result has been an agency that runs efficiently with employees empowered to present ideas, knowing that any appropriate suggestion will be taken seriously. I freely admit that I don't have all the good ideas and greatly appreciate it when staff members provide valuable input. Indeed, we have obtained several grants because of employee suggestions and have also been able to streamline some of our activities.

Situational Management Style

When I first started working in one of the many part-time jobs that helped me pay for college, I really didn't have a management style. I doubt anyone does in that situation.

After all, few of us start at the top of the management chart. I guess if my father had been the head of a company, I might have begun my career with a title, but he worked for the NYC Department of Sanitation. An honorable job (one that afforded me opportunities), but it's not a job with much emphasis on upward mobility.

As a result, I did what most people do: I learned by watching. I had some management background simply from shepherding my siblings about. At the same time, I saw in my immediate family how my grandmother, as matriarch of our extended family, provided leadership, as did my mother. I didn't think of their actions as a management style—the concept was still being born in my mind—but that's what it was. They commanded with their presence, their awareness of everything that was happening in the home and outside, and their concern for the welfare of their f amily members.

From there, I became aware of professors who could guide a classroom rather than dictate to it. I moved on to watching the district attorney and how he kept multiple high-energy and focused professionals—all with diverse agendas and multiple cases—functioning smoothly. Other leaders offered clear images of what not to do. In many ways, that's also very important; role models don't always have to be positive.

For example, I consciously chose to avoid certain lifestyle choices, such as drugs, by observing how people behaved on the street near our apartment. They were slovenly and callous.

They smoked, drank, used drugs, and generally hung around idly. I refused to live like that. I deliberately dressed as well as I could, worked on building a good vocabulary, and established career goals. I was determined not to end up living an unproductive life. Equally, I was an example for my brothers and sisters. As a result, they now own their own businesses or are doing well as employees in various lines of work.

When we were kids at home, I could be direct and almost dictatorial. That style would not work at EDCSPIN, however, where I was trying to build consensus. Managers have to be concerned more about their staff and the organization than their own needs. That requires them to be flexible to match the requirements of the job.

That's why some coaches are successful, while others are not. A young team that needs discipline will not respond to a laissez-faire manager, though a veteran team may. Many times, a leader must shift from one style to another for best results.

Leadership Styles

In his seminal book *Primal Leadership*, internationally known psychologist and former *New York Times* science reporter Daniel Goleman identified six different styles of leadership:

1. Visionary: explaining and guiding in a new direction;
2. Coaching: helping employees improve by connecting goals to performance;

3. Affiliative: building teamwork;

4. Democratic: encouraging staff input;

5. Pacesetting: setting standards; and

6. Commanding: controlling and dictating.

These styles all have strengths and limitations. For example, the visionary style works best when the organization is changing, but it can limit action. It can also cause problems if the new path isn't clearly understood by everyone. Coaching can really help employees, unless they feel they are being micromanaged or don't believe the coach is qualified. The affiliative method reduces conflicts and provides motivation; however, staff have to believe in the leader. If EDCSPIN employees did not accept me, they would not follow my plan.

The democratic concept allows input, but it both slows decision making when action is needed and fails completely when close supervision is required. Our agency was not ready for democracy when I took over, so I waited to implement it. Pacesetting works well with highly motivated staffers who don't need tremendous oversight. However, it can doom morale by causing employees who fail to reach the high bar to feel like failures. It also causes problems when teams are working on projects, because someone in the group may fall short.

Commanding remains popular but really works only

when immediate decisions are needed. Otherwise, it can undercut job satisfaction, particularly when the "commander" is a despot.

Success requires finding the right fit at the right time. In my case, when I was called into the agency, action was needed to right the boat and to reassure the employees. I could not wait for input or simply dictate. Instead, I articulated the vision of the agency and encouraged team building. From there, I moved into the democratic approach, seeking ideas from my staff.

I believe any leader must be flexible that way. Success comes by recognizing when one approach isn't working and another should be tried. Furthermore, each style has these three internal elements: Directing, Discussing, and Delegating.

Directing

The directing element of management has to be professional, concise, and direct. Employees must know what's happening. Failure to communicate invites rumors, which can quickly erode any progress.

A leader cannot abdicate his or her role. I couldn't let someone else conduct the first meeting; the staff would have figured that I was only a figurehead. Any information to the staff in the form of email and directives also had to carry my name. I had to direct. Then my job was to tell an employee what to do and how to do it. Communication was one-way:

from me to the staff. It had to be precise and provide an overview of my thinking. That established my credibility to lead the agency. As I mentioned earlier, employees need the important details, but they don't need to be bogged down with excessive facts that can confuse the situation. This approach worked very well when I first arrived but was quickly abandoned so that skilled staffers did not feel micromanaged.

Discussing

The discussion element of management followed. In the private meetings and later in large-group sessions, I invited employees to provide their input; I became a facilitator. This works by asking questions, such as: "What could have been done better?" "Do you have suggestions for how you can improve?" and so on. Here, I didn't want to dictate, but to encourage employees to find their path to improvements.

In group meetings, I knew what I wanted the staff to decide on a particular course of action and, through questions and suggestions, helped guide the decision. In other situations, employees came up with results that differed from what I thought was best but that turned out to be a great choice.

In all cases, discussions cannot be dominated by a few individuals—including the CEO. This has to be a democratic process where everyone feels free to provide input and is given the opportunity to do so. "What do you think?" is a great opener for any discussion.

Delegating

Finally, I learned to delegate and then let the designated employee do her job. This third internal element created empowerment. Employees then develop as individuals: improving, learning, and feeling more in control of their own careers. Most people learn best by doing. They cannot function, however, with someone breathing down their necks; they are afraid to be creative or to risk making a mistake.

Managers must make sure that each and every employee knows exactly what to do. Nebulous instructions can hamstring anyone. At the same time, dates need to be assigned for each deliverable. I set the schedule in accordance with the employee's expectations: When does he think he can finish a particular portion of the assigned task? Such deadlines need to be realistic but enforced.

Delegation leads to recognition. Someone who took on a task—such as organizing a special event or arranging for visitors to tour the agency—and handled it well deserves to be praised publicly. Private commendations are nice, but employees typically prefer that their peers know about their accomplishments. Donations may be given anonymously, but praise deserves an audience.

Employee Input Required

As you can tell, employee participation is the key to successful implementation of any style of leadership. Obviously, if staff members decline to get involved, any idea, no matter how good, will deflate quickly. That's also true if employees feel they cannot contribute.

In some management styles, such as the one I endured in Albany, no one is supposed to say anything; just listen and obey. But all that did was stifle creativity.

This problem is nationwide, by the way. A 2012 survey by Fierce, Inc., a communication training and leadership organization, found that many employees "believe many workplace practices aren't effective and often get in the way of performance results."[1] At the same time, nearly 50 percent of employees thought that management failure to explain how decisions are made and the lack of employee input hurt productivity. The solution is to ask employees to offer their ideas.

In the past, companies used to put out suggestion boxes. Then, on some undefined day, some boss wearily sat down and read the occasional entry. Often, the box was a repository for insults or isolated complaints. A few suggestions might even be anatomically impossible. The box also really didn't encourage participation, since everyone could see who was submitting the suggestion. Many employees resorted to early morning forays or other surreptitious methods of dropping a note in the box.

These days, the box seems so old-fashioned. With computers, any employee can quietly submit an idea or a comment without a colleague knowing about it. However, this approach is not completely anonymous, since the person reading the email knows where it came from.

An alternative is a survey. In this approach, the person reading the results has no idea who submitted them. This method is used at universities, where students can evaluate their instructors without fearing any repercussions. The survey is done online but does not record who filled it out.

Survey questions have to be carefully written if the results are to be useful. Questions that are too general won't provide the necessary feedback to help a manager address a situation. The type of questions also has to vary, perhaps including some with a five-point scale from very satisfactory to unsatisfactory and others that are open ended and require written feedback.

The survey can't be too long. Our clients need attention, and every minute that a staffer does something else detracts from services. Experts suggest that thirty-five to fifty-five questions are sufficient. Regardless, any survey shouldn't take more than twenty-five minutes to complete. More than that, and the process seems like an imposition.

A good survey should garner up to 90 percent participation. I use staff meetings before work to hand out surveys and let employees fill them out. Some employees who miss the meeting can fill the survey out later and place it in a receptacle so I don't know who answered the questions.

Surveys are not the only option. These days, any organization can set up an online site where employees can leave messages and suggestions. They can identify themselves or remain anonymous. Then, too, there's always the suggestion box; modern technology hasn't replaced it entirely yet.

Any request for information or ideas creates an implied commitment from management to follow up. My employees need to know their voices are heard. Josh Greenberg, president of AlphaMeasure, a research firm based in Boulder, Colorado, noted that "If you're going to collect all this data and then not close the loop back to the employees it almost makes sense not to do the survey. It's important to let them know that they've been heard."[2]

I use meetings to introduce changes or new plans based on the surveys and suggestions I've received. By making public announcements at group meetings, agency employees know that I care about their input from surveys or suggestions. Nothing falls flatter than a survey without the backing of management.

Once employees see that a leader is serious about making improvements and that positive changes are being made, they begin to feel empowered. They begin to coalesce into a team.

Briefly stated, here are the steps I followed to achieve that goal:

◇ Create a vision.
◇ Define everyone's role within that vision.

- Set long-term and short-term goals.
- Clearly communicate the vision and goals.
- Set a schedule and stick to it.
- Ask for input and accept criticism and advice.
- Don't expect immediate results; change takes time.
- Recognize employees who achieve set goals.
- Always encourage.
- Be flexible.
- Delegate.

It worked at my agency. Within a year after taking over at EDCSPIN, I could see that attitudes had shifted. That reality is clearly visible on the bottom line: Today, EDCSPIN has a $25 million annual budget and more than five hundred employees. Every one of them is doing a great job.

As steel magnate Andrew Carnegie said: "Teamwork is the ability to work together toward a common vision; the ability to direct individual accomplishments toward organizational objectives. It is the fuel that allows common people to attain uncommon results."[3]

I really believe it was the turning point of my life when I took this large group of people, many of whom resented me because I replaced their beloved director and none of whom had a real bond with one another, and turned them into a meaningful team that is paddling together and enthusiastically working for the community.

◆ ◆ ◆

Alfredo Giovine's "Perspective" essay explains the traditional Italian background he came from and built on. He discusses his core values, the qualities he looks for in his staff, and how he was able to develop his restaurant business and make it an integral part of the community in Barbados.

PERSPECTIVE: TAPAS WITH A VIEW

Alfredo Giovine, Owner, Tapas Restaurant,
Barbados, West Indies

I was born in the south of Italy, in Bari. In Italy, you finish your secondary school at eighteen and then you go to university. Fortunately, I had the opportunity to get admitted into a very popular academy in Milan.

When I moved to Milan, I started to live on my own. That, of course, was a big difference because you start to be responsible for your own life. You can eat when you want; you can sleep when you want; you do your foolishness and partying; but again you are responsible. I took university very seriously, but I saw friends go back home after the first year because life in another city by yourself can be rather challenging.

I graduated with a degree in economics. I never had

any experience with restaurants or the food business because it was never my first interest. I ended up living in Colombia for almost two years by chance, because I got a job distributing Italian food and products. That was my first contact with the food business. When I came to Barbados, it was because I was partnering with other people who were opening an Italian restaurant, and that became the first commercial experience I had in the food business.

I cannot say restaurants were my life. I ended up in the restaurant business because I liked the relationships with the people. I also like it because it is labor intensive. You open every day for many hours per day—it's not nine to five—and then you go home. And even when I go home, I still have to check what's going on with the business.

Of course, because it's mine I want to make sure everything goes well, but I also really like to be sure all my customers are happy. For example, if I make a special pasta just for you that is not on the menu, you feel very honored and happy. For me, it's nothing major: I have the kitchen; I have the products in the fridge. Just give me the time to cook it, and I will make you happy. The different perspective is amazing. For me, it's my daily job. For you, it's like "Wow, Alfredo made pasta dishes just for me."

So, you can really and truly make people happy

without a big effort; that's my bottom line. I always tell the guys, "I want whoever leaves this establishment to leave happy." I want my employees to embrace that goal and work together to achieve it.

When I hire staff—waiters, hosts, bartenders—I look to see if you are naturally nice. If you are, you can learn how to do this job. Serving people is not hard: You learn how to pour the wine; you learn where to put the cups. But to really be nice, to smile at people, to be pleasant—you cannot train or create that; it has to be inside. I have to find people who like to share most of their time with other people. You have to be committed to the goal of customer satisfaction, and you have to care about their dining experience.

Having the opportunity to travel has always been something that I liked. And for me, travel means going somewhere, meeting the people of that place, spending my time with them, and sharing as much as I can of my experience and their experience. I brought new things to Barbados, but Barbados also had a lot of things that were new to me. It's a reciprocal sharing of experience.

For example, when people asked me about Italian wine or food, I realized that even though I never studied it, I knew a lot because I lived it, watching TV, hearing my parents talk. So, I have a lot of knowledge about wine and food, not because I was reading it in books or studying it but simply because I experienced it in my environment.

I have lived in a number of places—South America, Venezuela, Costa Rica, and Italy—and I have traveled a lot through Europe and the United States. I have already spent ten years in Barbados, and I can say that I have decided to live out my life here.

The culture in Barbados is a very level playing field: businessmen sharing their experience with ordinary people or paying their own bills in the supermarket line. The other day, a government minister was standing in line in front of me at the supermarket. In Italy, privilege is everywhere—because I am so-and-so, I don't go to the supermarket and buy my own cigarettes. But here, at the end of the day, people live their lives as they see fit. So, I find the society here very fair and very honest.

I grew up in a family where everyone had plenty of freedom to think about the future without the pressure of expectations. For example, my dad graduated in pharmacology but ended up being a writer and opened his own publishing house. I come from a background where people are doing what they really feel they need to do; I've never been stuck in a specific career track.

I came to Barbados because I received a call that there was an Italian couple the same age as my mom and dad who were opening a delicatessen, and they were looking for somebody to help them run this place. I had met them when I was distributing food products and living in Colombia. They asked if I was interested, and at the time, I was just finishing my internship in Colombia. I decided I'd go to Barbados for a few months to help these people open their business.

I had to learn to deal with customers on a day-to-day basis, and that's when I realized I really liked it. The couple who were my business partners helped me a lot. First of all, because they were my parents' age, they took me in and treated me like their son, for which I was really grateful. They were very kind, and I learned a lot from them, and of course, I gave them all my energy and passion.

Mama Mia was a typical Italian deli, offering pasta, pizza, and sandwiches, with all the ingredients brought in from Italy. The deli was very successful because it was something new for Barbados at a time when Bajans (Barbadians) started to open up to different types of food. Bajans have started to travel more and experience different foods. That was one of the key elements that made Mama Mia a success.

I ran Mama Mia for six years for the couple. Then, in 2009, two other Italian guys who were living here and I took over and reopened as Tapas. We refreshed the place, which has a very nice spot right in front of the ocean, and we made a good deal with the previous management and landlord. After six months, one of the three who was less involved realized it made no sense to stay, so we bought him out. Now it is just two of us: the chef and me. One runs the kitchen; the other runs the floor. We share all the duties and responsibilities equally, so each one does his part. The great thing is that each of us has a very high respect for the other. I don't step into the kitchen and say, "I know this should have more salt or be served with this sauce." I simply pass on my advice or suggestions and what I hear on the floor: "Yes, people like it," or "No, they don't like it." But if I have a problem with the kitchen staff, though I am an owner of the business, I don't go and deal with the kitchen staff. I tell my partner, Franco, "John had this problem yesterday," or "I had this problem with John. You sort it out. It's your guy." This way, we maintain the reputation and respect that the two of us have with the relative staff.

Whatever happens on the floor is my responsibility; whatever happens in the kitchen is his. This has been a key point for me. You manage your duties and responsibilities, and you know that you are the only chief in your area. I think that in this kind of environment you need to have a very clear chain of command because, at the end of the day, it is the kind of business where problems have to be solved extremely quickly. For example, if a customer complains about a dish, I don't have the time to say, "Come tomorrow and I will give you some different food." The customer is looking for a solution now. So, for me, it is very important that the roles and responsibilities are clear to everybody so that everyone knows where to go and how to operate.

We have sixty people employed at Tapas, and our common goal is to provide a great customer experience. To achieve that goal, we must be clear when giving direction and assigning tasks. Managing sixty people in a fixed space requires excellent choreography, so it is especially important that each person moves in the same direction, toward the same goal. At Tapas, we try to do this in ways that reflect the proud culture of Barbados.

For example, people here are very honest and hospitable. Barbados is the kind of place where if your wallet falls out of your pocket 95 percent of people will pick it up to give it back to you exactly as you lost it. One of the other things that also impress tourists is that if you stop on the road and ask for directions, many times people will say, "Follow me." It's a very friendly place. So, of course, we want our restaurant to reflect that as well.

To give you an idea, one night just after we first opened Tapas, during closing I forgot to shut the main door. Because we went out the back door, the main door was left open, and I didn't realize it. At 2:00 a.m., a policeman came to my house—it's a small island, so the policeman knew where I lived—and said, "Alfredo, there is a problem at Tapas. Come with me."

When I got there, I realized the door was open. I had left the restaurant at around 11:00 p.m., and for three or four hours anyone could have helped themselves to all the liquor and spirits, but no one took anything. Someone called the police and said, "Look, Tapas is open, and no one is there." There are many more stories like this.

Right in front of the restaurant there is a boardwalk that the city built a few years ago. That has become a very nice location, because it is the only place on the island that you can really walk along the ocean without cars passing. Coming from a city in the south of Italy, I enjoy regular strolls along the ocean, just meeting friends and having a beer on the plaza—a meeting place like residents enjoyed in Roman and Greek times. That is what I imagined would happen with this boardwalk, and that is what it has become now.

I have a slice of Barbados passing in front of me every day. It not only helps my business, but it also helps my relationships with people. One day you have a little one who wants a glass of water, and another day someone has a small accident and needs rubbing alcohol for his knee. They are small things, but they foster the sense of family, of community, where everyone is there for one another.

This kind of togetherness, where everyone helps one another, is important to Barbadians. We understand that we are all in this thing called life together, and we'll all prosper if we work together toward a common goal.

PERSPECTIVE: LEADING THROUGH UNCERTAINTY

Carla D. Brown, Executive Director, Walburg Center

Providing services to the most vulnerable New Yorkers and often overlooked citizens—seniors—has been an honor for me. As a first-generation American of Panamanian ancestry, I was lucky enough to grow up with my maternal grandparents in the home I shared with my parents. My strength and faith come from the lessons that I learned from these immigrants who arrived in the U.S. to build on a dream for success. My grandmother, a woman of profound faith, pre-deceased my grandfather the year before I graduated from college, first in my immediate family. My grandfather died on the day I started this job; it felt as if caring for the well-being of seniors was a baton he handed to me. I had spent the better part of six months caring for him while he was in the hospital battling congenital heart failure.

Believe it or not, COVID-19 is not the first emergency situation that I have had to lead my organization through. The first was 9/11, and the second was Hurricane Sandy. While the days that ensued were challenging and often eventful, we made it out. This global pandemic still continues with no end in sight and no time to find a new normal as things shift and change each day. Imagine hearing the mayor of NYC imploring all New Yorkers to stay home but being told that your homebound delivered meals program was deemed essential? In the first two weeks, several staff members walked off the job because they expressed concern about contracting the illness. Soon after, others left to collect the increased unemployment benefits that were provided. As it happened, I was called to lead in the most basic of ways and that was to drive and deliver meals. As a woman in a male-dominated occupation, an impact was made when I appeared stronger than they imagined and unafraid. Well, I was more afraid than they knew, but I was clear about the importance of creating a sense of normalcy for the people who depended on us.

The city agency that contracted us announced that they would fund our programs with emergency COVID-19 funds until the end of the fiscal year, June 30th. It was clear to everyone in NYC, which at the outset was hit the hardest by this pandemic, that we would still be in crisis on and after July 1st. We could not spare time off for staff, as the number of seniors we serviced grew by 30 percent in a three-week period. Using my community connections, I was able to get volunteers from various civic organizations to join us on Saturdays to ease the load on the weekends. Those connections grew into several Saturday volunteer activities and fundraising efforts totaling over $4,000 for PPE equipment for staff. It also allowed for an opportunity to educate others about the needs of the elders that we serve. Today, over a year later, we are still coordinating with groups that want to give back and assist our day-to-day programming.

Yes, a year later, with a staff turnover of almost 65 percent, there is still no end in sight. While staff that were furloughed were calling our senior center partici- pants and homebound seniors to encourage them to get vaccinated, I completed the two-dose Pfizer vaccine in February. I announced it to a largely skeptical staff and had to impress upon them that while they had spent the better part of a year fighting food insecurity and isola- tion, it meant nothing if they were not willing to first care for themselves in a tangible way. More than 40 percent of the staff has been vaccinated to date, while others have secured appointments. I hope to get that number to 100 percent. There is now talk about new strains of the virus and booster vaccines on the horizon, and there seems to be no end in sight.

Leading through the unknown means your compass is your mission and purpose. In the very early months, when we were short-staffed and delivering meals past 6 p.m., the gratefulness of the seniors when we arrived meant that we were successful. They were in awe as we showed up day after day to feed them and ensure their safety. I am the Cheerleader-in-Chief, and I celebrate my staff as the true heroes that they are. They all played and continue to exercise huge roles during this season. We are pushing through because our committed service has literally saved lives.

In the midst of the turmoil, I wrote a proposal to contract with the city for another few years, developing a plan in which funding was based on pre-COVID NYC. In each and every line, I did my best to capture what we do, but most of all, how why we do it in spite of the unexpected. The sacrifice has been great but worth it. The legacy of the community that we serve has been preserved. We were awarded the new contract but the programmatic and fiscal uncertainty remained. We don't know what tomorrow will hold but we know what happens if we keep going.

Leading through crisis without knowing where and when it will end takes more courage than I ever thought it would. Whatever comes your way, your faith and strength grow as you survive another day. It's what my family did over fifty years ago when they arrived in this country. The success of this organization is a reflection of the lessons my grandparents taught me.

PERSPECTIVE: THE PURPOSE JOURNEY

PK Kersey, Husband, Father, Speaker, Author, and
President and Founder, That Suits You

Every few years a new word or term dominates people searching for success. Purpose is currently that term. Walk in your purpose. Be in your purpose. Don't live a life without purpose. But what does that truly mean? For years I had no idea. People might have thought I did because I was a minister in a church and I used to teach about it so often. That was the really strange thing is that I thought I knew what it meant. I truly did. I would teach about how important it was and that every human had a God-given responsibility to find purpose. I would even say that we robbed ourselves when we refused to walk in our purpose because God needed us to. Wow, just hearing that excites me. The only unfortunate thing about that is I had no clue what it meant.

I grew up in East New York, Brooklyn, NY—a very tough part of the city to say the least. I was a very dedicated follower. In other words, I did whatever my friends did or told me to do. I lacked confidence growing up, so I depended on my friends for security and comfort. No matter how bad the decisions or choices they made, I was committed to following them. I just thank God my lack of confidence didn't have tragic results because I really made some horrible choices. I can't even say I made terrible choices because the choices were really made by my friends. I just went along with them without questioning anything. Just thinking about it now, I can see how sad and dangerous that was. However, this was who I was.

As a child, I was fortunate to have both parents in my household. I say fortunate because most of my friends had only one parent or they lived with their grandparents. So, having both was definitely a blessing. Growing up, my parents taught me, my sister, and my brother their idea for success: work hard, save, retire from your employer, and live comfortably. It worked great for them. They had their struggles, but overall they lived a blessed life. So as good parents, they shared their path with their children. My mother worked for Verizon for over thirty years and retired. My father worked for NYC Transit for twenty-seven years and retired. Perfect! Like I said, it worked great for them. I in turn listened to them and worked for NYS DMV for twenty-four years and was well on my way to retiring when I began to feel a sense of emptiness. I followed their path to a T but did not feel the same sense of accomplishment in my life that they felt in theirs. I didn't know what it was, but I knew I wasn't living to my fullness. So even though I spoke about it and thought I had it, I was far away from living in my purpose.

I often liken it to the movie *The Matrix*, when Morphius is trying to explain the Matrix to Neo and tells him, "I cannot tell you what the Matrix is, I have to show you!" It is very difficult to tell someone about their purpose; they have to walk into it themselves. Being married, having kids, working for the DMV, and remaining very involved in the church all may have been a part of being in my purpose or all may have helped lead me to my purpose, but I do not feel I had really begun to walk in my purpose until I stepped outside of my comfort zone.

That feeling of knowing you have more to offer and actually doing it is a very special moment in the purpose journey. It is like all the gender reveals we see going on with new parents to see what is the gender of their child. The purpose reveal is a very special and exciting time. It is exciting but also scary because it really hits you like WOW! If your purpose doesn't scare you, then you may still not know what it is. One day while pondering my future in disappointment, I received a word from God like BOOM . . . I want you to collect suits and give them to men all over the country so that they can get back to work! Just hearing that statement sends chills to my spine because I know how I felt when I initially heard it. It was extremely powerful and has changed my entire life. Up until that day I had never even really thought about anything like that or felt I had the capacity to carry it out. I figured how could I, a follower, a DMV employee fulfill such a calling? Little did I know that all along it was all inside me; I just didn't believe it.

Once that word hit my spirit I began planning, strategizing, and speaking to people who I felt could make this a reality. The first time in my life I felt I was leading and not following for a change. I was in the leadership position. I felt a purpose inside of me to accomplish this and make moves. I quickly realized that purpose is more so for other people than it is for yourself. Now, of course you will benefit from using your gifts and talents, but the overall community and others will benefit greatly. Isn't that what life is about anyway, helping others to be better? To date www.thatsuitsyou.org has assisted over ten thousand individuals, authored four books, and provided workshops and clothing. We have been featured on several news outlets and magazines. I mention this to say that purpose is a very powerful thing, and when you enter into it, your life will never be the same.

PERSPECTIVE: STRATEGIC PARTNERS

Dr. Laura Zumdahl, President and CEO, New Moms

Several years after moving the headquarters of the organization I lead, New Moms, to a neighborhood on the West Side of Chicago from an area closer to the center, we noticed a consistent increase in demand for our programs and services for young moms and their children from communities outside the city boundary. We were, geographically, only a mile from the edge of the city, and suburban young moms were seeking the same supports we offered to those in the city.

This data point was a nudge for us to think about our strategy for geographic expansion as our organization grew. One counterpoint to the demand we were seeing was an agency in the adjacent town that provided similar services to the same population. While smaller and not meeting all the needs, our entry into that community would be deemed as overlap, which did not seem like the best use of resources.

As I considered options for navigating this, I reached out to introduce myself to the relatively new executive director of the neighboring agency. Over breakfast we talked shop and about our respective organizations. Picking up on the subtext of the conversation, I gently asked if they had ever thought about partnering with a larger organization to help deal with some of the fund-raising and scale challenges they were encountering. She bristled at the question and quickly assured me they had it all under control.

Feeling like that path had a dead-end, I dismissed the notion and New Moms continued to focus on our work in the city and let the lingering question about expanding our geography linger for the time being. About six months later, I received a call from that same executive director asking to meet again. Over lunch she confided that her organization was not, in fact, fine. They had lost a major contract, which called into question their long-term survival. Compelled by the great need for their mission, but at a loss for finding a sustainable model, she thought of our conversation and reached out to see if we might consider acquiring the organization.

While the door to a strategic partnership opened in that conversation, it was not easy to say "yes" yet. We embarked on a significant learning process to understand the organization and their model over the next few months. Several honest, and at times hard, conversations were part of that process. It was a bit like dating—we were feeling each other out to see if there was enough chemistry to make a long-term commitment.

One lesson from leading during this time was the need to balance an openness to another way of doing things and the culture and quirks of another organization with holding tight when I needed to draw lines in the sand. In negotiating an acquisition agreement, I was keenly aware we had the upper hand at New Moms. We were bigger and would be the surviving organization. Without this partnership, the smaller organization would probably cease to exist. But they came into the arrangement with a lot of requests that we had to listen to and respect. And while some of those requests we could grant, there were others that we could not. I had to be clear about our organization's culture and values and what would happen after the acquisition so there were no surprises later.

Course correcting for them was to ensure their mission would endure beyond the organization by folding into another organization. While this was a win for them (especially in comparison to the alternative of extinction), it was not easy and without accepting some realities of what a partnership like this would look like.

In the end we worked through the questions, signed a formal agreement, and began the process of integration of the two organizations. It took several years to really make the cultural integration complete, but because of the thoughtfulness and intentionality we put into the process, we emerged stronger together and with the benefit of a larger geographic area to serve. It solved a problem for New Moms and for the other organization while putting us on a course to achieve our mission in greater ways.

Principle Six

EVERY CREW MEMBER MATTERS

My individual interviews with EDCSPIN employees went well, for the most part. I understood they would be nervous, but I expected them to treat me with respect. Only a couple of people were what I considered rude. One young man, for example, sauntered in, draped himself over the chair, and paid little attention to anything I said.

Over time, I have learned that his behavior, while inappropriate, was not unique. In every company or organization, there are invariably a few people who don't seem to fit in or even want to. They usually don't last long, but I encourage leaders to tolerate that kind of behavior from individuals who are also making valuable contributions. (I don't advocate total insubordination or rudeness, of course, no matter how productive the individual.) Otherwise, we risk draining the creativity that often comes with slightly unusual behavior. For example, with someone who's very productive, you might overlook the occasional late arrival to work, unconventional clothing or hairstyle, the tendency to chat a bit too long with coworkers, and the like. But not to the point of allowing them to flout the rules or of showing favoritism that others could complain about.

Address Difficult People

Here are some of the difficult staffers I've had to deal with and the course I chose in handling each person's challenges:

Egotists. These folks think they are special. So, they tend to shun time clocks and take breaks whenever the urge appears. Their work is often excellent, though, and as a result, I want them to stay. But I don't want the headaches they cause. Their behavior can lead to two problems: First, their demands can get excessive, overshadowing value. Second, other employees may chafe when they see someone getting special benefits. I try to treat everyone the same, but demands of certain jobs require them to be there when the front door opens. In one particular case, I had to reprimand a perpetually late prima donna, which undermined his enthusiasm. I didn't want him to quit, so finally we discussed ways to resolve the concern. I then put him in a position where flexible hours were part of the job. (This highlights the difference between having hourly workers and salaried ones. Salaried workers might work sixty hours a week yet be paid for only forty, but they might be allowed some flexibility in their work schedule where permitted. Hourly workers usually do not have flexible schedules.) He has been very good since then.

Not doing anything would not have helped. Inactivity creates a vicious circle, with resentment rising as the prima donna follows her or his own rules. That in turn undermines trust between management and staff. Trust is a key component in any organization's success, so as a result, most of us would be better off without such individuals. Stars may drive the worlds of sports and entertainment, but once they enter the working world, they need to fit in for the benefit of everyone. If my prima donna hadn't adjusted and accepted the new job, I would have reluctantly asked him to leave.

Nitpickers. Some people want everything to be perfect. That's helpful as long as it doesn't interfere with production. But when someone quibbles over every aspect of a project, there can be problems, as well as a real dilemma. We each want whatever we do to represent our best work; consequently, we want to correct any mistakes. At the same time, however, we face deadlines for grant submissions and other projects. We had a nit-picking perfectionist at the agency who was causing havoc with our ability to submit applications and other documents on time. My first choice was to discuss the deadlines with everyone and to be sure there was ample time to meet them. I also assigned the perfectionist to help with the planning, but kept her away from the final process. Of course, we could have made sure every project was completed perfectly, but that's improbable. We simply do the best we can. We focus on finding and correcting major errors, not every mistake.

Innovators. These people are always thinking ahead but get distracted from the job at hand. For example, I have an employee who is extraordinarily creative. She has found ways of streamlining several processes, and I don't want to discourage her. After all, ideas are the lifeblood of any organization. On the other hand, today's work has to be done. She wasn't completing anything because she was so busy coming up with new ways to do something. That, in turn, antagonized her colleagues, who were forced to do her work as well as their own. My answer was to create an outlet for her to submit ideas. We would talk about them, and at the same time, I carefully monitored her assigned tasks, making sure they were completed as required and on time. She got the hint soon enough, and I have ended up with a valuable employee.

Create a Process

In each situation I just described, I followed a clear process that was obvious to the staff. It told everyone that creativity would be rewarded but that anything that damaged the agency or created turmoil among employees would not be acceptable. The steps in the process provided tactics for dealing with problem employees, allowing me to isolate the concern and reduce the chances that the employee's negative traits and behaviors would infect the rest of the agency.

Communicate. This mutes the grousing, prunes back the grapevine, and shuts down the rumor mill. I always keep my door open and immediately let employees know what is happening that affects them. Material is posted on the website, sent in email to employees, and, if necessary, posted in writing. There's no reason for any employee not to know the truth. This was vitally important when I became the director; I had to stifle claims that people would be fired or jobs would be eliminated. It also strengthened my position when none of the negative rumors proved to be true and the communication from my office was accurate.

Be active. I can't just sit in my office. I walk around; I talk to employees. They know I'm the leader and may not be in a position to be completely open about everything that's going on in the background; however, the more they see me and realize that we're working together, the more they are willing to tell me their concerns. I want them to raise any concerns to me, not simply spout objections into the office where they can infect others.

Outline the procedure. The staff need to know that inappropriate negative comments or the spreading of false reports has consequences. I don't expect everything to be rosy all the time, but I do expect concerns to be channeled through the right process so they can be addressed. Employees who fail to follow the channels can expect reprimands based on a clearly stated procedure.

Get good employees. That's really the best choice. Hire people with positive attitudes; that is, the kind who don't carp but look for solutions. Following this broad approach, I have greatly reduced negativity at the agency, enabling us to focus on helping our clients. Unfortunately, I haven't reached everyone; no one can. There are always some employees who test limits, violate basic rules, and generally cause havoc through actions, words, or both. Dealing with them has required a very different process.

I certainly do not get involved in personnel matters unless the situation is significant. I don't want to hold a formal, in-office meeting with someone who is upset over something minor. A brief conversation in the hallway suffices.

For the more significant breaches, I have to be sure the employees were really exhibiting bad behavior. After all, something I think is unacceptable may seem perfectly normal to someone else. It's easy to misunderstand. I can't even count the number of times I misconstrued something only because I heard part of a conversation or saw some gesture out of context. I am sure everyone else has had similar experiences.

Besides, people have different upbringings and culture. Sometimes, I just have to whisper a comment to someone to eliminate the problem. I don't want to embarrass the person, but I want the particular action stopped.

Determine Guidelines: Results Matter

Sometimes, a simple example takes care of the problem. Everyone needs guidelines. The easiest solution is simply letting someone know how I want the phone answered or the best way to deal with an overbearing parent. I do not accept any finger-pointing or excuses. The cause of a problem does not matter; staff will simply need to work out a solution that ends the disruptions. The agency's expectations must be respected. If I have a choice, I will always opt for the simplest option, the one with the fewest disruptions in the agency's life and the one that preserves the employee's job.

For example, two squabbling employees can create turmoil in an office. Because of their jobs, they regularly interact, but their bickering is cutting into productivity and annoying their colleagues. My approach is to speak directly to both of them, letting them know that their petty difference cannot be allowed to undermine their work. I expect them to be responsible and professional while on the job. Of course, they will be told that further disruptions could have serious consequences.

The point is to address the situation quickly and firmly. Any misbehaving employees need to understand what is expected of them while working for the agency. They may need some coaching to learn new strategies. For instance, new employees may never have worked in an agency or had to function on teams before. My role then is to encourage the employees while carefully monitoring progress. People are held accountable for their actions, but they must know which actions are inappropriate and must be changed.

This can be a lengthy process, but any employee deserves the opportunity unless the behavior is particularly egregious, such as stealing or physically attacking someone else. I create a timetable with milestones the employee is expected to reach en route to a change in behavior. That may include counseling sessions, training, or just a commitment to learn office procedures.

The employee may be asked to apologize to the offended parties, just to help rebuild trust and camaraderie. That's a hard step for anyone but also an indication of a willingness to improve.

Of course, I can't be naïve. Some people will say all the right things and do the opposite. Nevertheless, with the proper approach, I have been able to retain good employees and eliminate inappropriate behavior.

Typically, the infighting and loud arguments are rare and can be handled swiftly. Unfortunately, not everything is that smooth, especially when a serious breach of agency rules occurs. In such a circumstance, everyone is watching to see what happens. Will I uphold the rules, especially if an important worker is involved? The answer is important. Other employees usually don't like to endure misbehaving colleagues for very long. They also lose respect when the rules aren't applied equally.

My only choice, then, is to follow a set process that the employees are informed of when hired. It's part of their employment manual and explained in meetings.

They face meetings and official reprimands following violation of known company policy and other major transgressions. For example, an employee who steals from his colleagues creates a dangerous situation for clients. Someone who misrepresents himself, fails to file the necessary reports, makes false claims for insurance purposes, or performs similar misdeeds also falls into that category. Major misbehavior like that requires immediate, decisive intervention.

Documentation is important, both for fairness and for legal concerns. The employees need to know that everyone is treated fairly and equally. Documentation helps show that the correct action was taken and that it was consistent from one staffer to the next. Privacy laws prevent sharing the information, but everyone knows when I ask someone to leave that I have sufficient evidence and cause.

At the same time, as a lawyer, I am well aware that the agency could end up in court if a former employee felt discriminated against or unfairly fired. The documents amassed in an employee file provide a legal basis for any action I take.

Regardless of what I think I should do, I always meet with any employee who has committed a serious transgression. I make sure either the employee's supervisor and/or the head of human resources joins us. That way, the session won't descend into a shouting contest. I rarely get upset, but any person called into a serious, employment-related meeting with a boss can get accusatory.

The usual problems are related to trust. Unfortunately, many people are wary of trusting others. They build walls and lash out inappropriately. They don't want anyone to "intrude" into their workspace or activities. They think the worst: Something will be said or done to hurt them—something will be misconstrued. They want to be appreciated and thanked, but instead, they create an atmosphere that causes the opposite results. So, they get to see me.

Firing really has to be the last step. As we all know, it takes time and money to hire and train a replacement. One lengthy study demonstrated that companies pay 20 percent of a worker's salary to replace her. That includes the loss of productivity while waiting for the replacement to get up to speed.

Considering how often people change jobs in a normal economy, it's always a good idea, then, to retain good workers. I hope this process helps a "problem child" learn the errors of his ways and straighten out.

Elements of the Resolution

Our agency's process, which I just outlined, has some easily discernible elements.

- ◇ **Be open and honest.** Examples help illustrate the concern. Many times employees are really bewildered about why I am disappointed about something they did. The event didn't register with them. A reminder helps.

◇ **Obtain all points of view.** If the meeting is in regard to a major upheaval, then I want to know what happened from the employee's point of view and from the perspective of everyone involved. This testimony helps create a clear picture in situations where I did not witness the event or have only a written complaint from a client's family to go on.

◇ **Ask what message the employee was sending.** If his plan was to be belligerent, then the path to discuss proper behavior is open. There's a psychological aspect here: We all have self-concepts. We all see ourselves one way and want others to see us that way. Employees see themselves as good people. Any discussion that explains how they allowed themselves to be seen differently can have an impact on future behavior.

◇ **Explain the impact.** Opportunities for raises and promotions often motivate staff members. Bad behavior can reduce those chances. Highlighting that reality often causes a slacker to rethink what happened and how it can hurt her in the future.

◇ **Provide alternatives.** An employee who feels frustrated and lashes out may not think of more orderly solutions, such as talking to personnel, a boss, or even me. I prefer that people use the chain of command, but I also understand that sometimes people want to go straight to the top. That's why my office door is always open. The point is to let any employee know there are good choices and bad ones. The hope is to nudge them toward making the good one. That involves providing the information needed to make the correct decision. Many of my employees work alone with clients. Confronted with a strange situation, they may not know what to do and may feel completely helpless. Bad decisions can be made in those situations. With information, the employee knows she is not isolated and that there is help.

⋄ **Be proactive.** I try to be aware of what's happening in the office. I want to try to cut off any problem before it arises. For example, if deadlines are approaching, staffers working on a project may be nervous and concerned. Frayed nerves can lead to confrontations. A respite at a restaurant, a chance to refresh and regroup, can help resolve a potential blowup before it happens.

⋄ **Listen to individual speech.** Sometimes the chronic complainer is speaking only for him- or herself, but there are times when the person might be reflecting the feelings of a whole department. That's why it's never a good idea to totally ignore the complaints. Check with colleagues and coworkers to see if there's any validity to the claims.

◇ **Be patient.** Change takes a while. Sometimes, a schedule is necessary: I may expect a medical report or completion of an anger-management program by a certain date, for example. That gives people room to work while reducing the stress related to uncertainty. After all, we are all works in progress. I always consider several points before taking any action: (1) Is the situation permanent, requiring action? Or will it slowly disappear? Most things just dissipate in time. (2) Does it really matter? Most problems really do not impact the agency or our ability to provide the needed service. As a result, I might be better off giving the air time to clear.

◇ **Be aware of other changes.** Now and again, employees feel threatened and act accordingly when conditions at work change or there's a shift in responsibilities. If the employee has been productive in the past, I will sit down with him and try to determine what the real problem is. Then, together we can come up with a solution.

◇ **Have witnesses.** I have to be careful to avoid the appearance of bias. As a result, I try to include the personnel director or a board member in an evaluation that could end in termination. I turn over all the notes and memos and encourage whoever sat in the meeting to offer an opinion. I still make the final decision, but input helps ensure that I make the appropriate one.

In the end, some employees will change and prove their value while others will have to leave. The young man who sprawled across the chair in our lone meeting, for instance, had to grow up somewhere else. By asking him to leave, I affirmed company values while setting a standard for everyone. The others who stayed after a meeting with me demonstrated that mistakes can be corrected, that everyone can learn, and that I want to do what is best for both the employee and the agency.

Those are valuable lessons that cut to the core of the agency's vision and create a lasting impression. Setting the bar high can be very valuable for ensuring a long-term and successful future.

◆　◆　◆

Guy Stanley Philoche, a painter, understands better than most the importance of each disparate element to the creation of a unified whole. In this final "Perspective" essay, he discusses his commitment to his work, touching on truth versus fame in the arts, his search for community, and above all, being true to oneself.

PERSPECTIVE: BEAUTIFUL ORGANIZATION OF CHAOS

Guy Stanley Philoche, Fine Art Painter, Paier College of Art

When I was a kid, I got lost in comic books and became a huge Disney fan. When everybody else went out to recess, I would get my comic book, read it, and try to copy everything. In my early childhood, I'd wake up and watch Disney cartoons while eating a big bowl of cereal. I wanted to create that world.

I realized I could draw really well when I was in the second or third grade. I drew a picture and the teacher asked me, "Did you trace that?"

I said, "What's tracing?"

She said, "Oh, wow, you can really draw."

But my big "Aha!" moment was probably going to the museums for the first time on a class trip and seeing the masterpieces—Picasso, van Gogh—all those greats. That's when I realized I wanted to be an artist. Ever since then, every time we had to do a report on someone, I always chose an artist. It was always about an artist that I loved.

After high school, once I got to art school, I met other people like myself, people who liked to draw. They weren't athletes or scholars, but I surrounded myself with people who could relate to me. That's one of the keys to success: surrounding yourself with people who are into the same things that you are into and who are all really positive. All that rubs off, and you feed off one another.

I remember my first big New York show. I sent a car to pick up my family in Connecticut. I remember my dad looking at my paintings, looking at the titles of everything, and he started noticing these little red dots next to the paintings. He asked me what the dots meant. I said, "It means they're sold." He was like, "Holy shit, you really are famous."

I said, "Not yet, but I'm working on it." That was probably one of the coolest moments: when my dad actually realized that this is what his son does—he's a painter.

But allow me to be super honest. Being an artist is not glamorous or sexy. I made tons and tons of sacrifices. All my friends are having kids and getting married, and I'm still just painting; I don't see myself doing anything else.

I've sold paintings because someone saw me delivering one on the subway. These are not urban legends; these are true stories that happen to real New Yorkers because your life really could change in a heartbeat. I always believed it was important to just keep your eye on the prize. I didn't come here to find love or to have a kid. I came for one purpose only: to be in the Museum of Modern Art.

One of the concepts of the "Everybody Paddles" movement that caught my attention was the notion of everybody pursuing a common goal. That's what I mean by keeping your eye on the prize. If you don't keep your eyes on your goal, it is easy to lose your way. My paintings are an attempt to bring order out of chaos in my own life. Even though I have pursued a career in which I work alone, I appreciate the importance of people working together as a community.

The community aspect in the art world is different. Working together as a community doesn't exist in the art world these days. It did back in the 1960s and 1970s, when Jackson Pollock and Jasper Johns looked out for each other. People are cutthroat now. I know super-famous artists, and I also know struggling artists. Famous artists are protective of their collectors' contacts; if they have any sense of competition, they feel you're stealing money from them. But in my case, every time I sell a painting, I tend to buy a painting from someone who is not well known.

People come to my studio and they ask, "Why do you collect art?" I believe in karma; you need to share love and look out for each other. For art to flourish, artists must also flourish, and the best way for that to happen is for artists to work together toward that common goal. Some of my work has been referred to as a "beautiful organization of chaos." I think there is something about the "Everybody Paddles" movement that speaks to that concept. It is a simple thing, but if we could remove the chaos of our everyday lives by simply working together, at the same time, toward a common goal, one can only imagine how beautiful our lives could be. That, to me, would be amazing.

PERSPECTIVE: COURAGE OF THE COLLECTIVE

Cy Jones, NFL Super Bowl Champion, Denver Broncos; and Founder, The Cy. Jones Foundation

What is courage? I'm willing to bet that if you asked ten people this question you would receive a variety of answers. Some quick, some more thought out. Deep answers along with answers that are simple and vague. *Webster's Dictionary* defines courage as "the mental or moral strength to venture, persevere, and withstand danger, fear, or difficulty." But what does that really mean? Truth is courage that is truly immeasurable and undefinable. Not in a sense that there aren't different levels to courage. But those levels are strictly and uniquely determined by each of us as individuals. The word itself can mean something different to everyone, therefore it is no true way of defining it. But courage is more than just a word. It is a feeling that determines a particular course of action. It's something that takes no skill, no money or special privilege to possess. To be courageous doesn't require any hours of special training, preparation, or practice. But yet it is something that we will all have the opportunity to display at some point in our lives. Courage directly correlates to our growth and success, and ultimately to those who depend on us. Especially when it relates to being a part of something greater than yourself. The elements that are required in order to be on a team or to work in a cooperative setting all require courage as a compass.

One of the most fundamental keys to having successful teamwork and consistent growth is authenticity. In a cooperative setting, in order to fully maximize operational potential, there must be full transparency between one another. This takes courage because as human beings we all have insecurities or things we don't necessarily favor about ourselves. Being open and displaying the most authentic version of ourselves leaves room for judgment/criticism, and that's what takes courage. Having the confidence to think and act as authentically as possible is very important in trying to accomplish anything with a group of people. Courage in authenticity provides the comfort for others to know exactly who and what they are getting when working with you in whatever role you serve. Courage in authenticity is made easier with proper attention to work environment. It is the responsibility of everyone, but more importantly leadership to provide a place where each person can maximize their courage. Being fully comfortable shows confidence, and being fully authentic is courageous.

Another aspect of courage that is essential to group success and collective achievement is accountability. Being able to accept responsibility is not always the easiest thing to do, specifically when it is about something negative or detrimental to the goal. But this could be argued as the most important aspect to accountability. When an individual has the courage to be accountable, this can clarify the origin of a problem. But also, it is the overall responsibility of everyone to make accountability second nature. Courage in accountability is crucial in eliminating time wasted and providing maximum time to provide solutions. Courage in accountability is what drives performance. Taking pride in your own performance and being able to critique your own mediocrity will directly increase productivity and keep standards high for the collective. Being able to hold oneself accountable is a true testament of courage, as it shows selflessness and commitment to excellence.

Having the courage to be accountable is ultimately the respect, pride, and belief in the standard.

One of the most underrated aspects of courage as it relates to cooperative settings is adaptation. The courage to adapt can make or break the flow and elevation of anything. Maneuvering through any type of change takes courage because it affects comfort and routine. Being fully comfortable has a direct effect on how well you perform and how well you are received by your peers, coworkers, and teammates. Courage in adaptation is setting aside the fear of change and relying on fundamentals and principles to return you to a place of familiarity. We are all better when we're most comfortable, but oftentimes the person who is able to adapt in any particular circumstance is the most successful. You are less flustered by change and therefore more able to think and act clearly, providing yourself and the others depending on you the assurance that you can perform even when your environment shifts.

So, there you have it! The three As in courage: authenticity, accountability, and adaptation. The decision to display each of these takes courage because it is simply difficult and undesirable. Being able to provide people with a fully transparent version of yourself is almost unrealistic, but the closer to 100 percent you reach in that effort is important. Unleashing your true self takes trust, and that is something that requires courage in itself. The more your peers, partners, or coworkers know you, the less they have to guess or be uncertain about what you can or cannot bring to the table. Authenticity provides clarification and leads to more efficiency. Being accountable displays personal pride in performance. The desire and commitment to achieve excellence and not settle for mediocrity is essential in finding success. Understanding the role you play in the collective, taking it seriously, and having substantial care in what you produce will provide maximum achievement—both personally and jointly. Last, adaptation allows for the consistent transition and flow from one thing to the next without setback. Achieving consistent success over a lengthy period of time requires flexibility—the wherewithal to uphold fundamentals and principles of old, while continuing to evolve with the nuances of whatever it is you're doing.

Regardless, the ultimate test of courage is putting aside the personal for the collective. The more authentic, accountable, and adaptive you are in your personal journey, the easier it will be to apply when others board the boat.

PERSPECTIVE: WHAT SUCCESSFUL LEADERS KNOW

Carine Jocelyn, CEO, Diaspora Community Services

Everybody Paddles. As simple and obvious as that sounds, it is a message that even the most experienced leaders sometimes forget. That statement is a reminder and acknowledgement that each individual member of an organization plays a role in its success. As in rowing, where the boat moves at the pace and direction of its leader or coxswain, the same is also true of an organization. And the similarities continue: the leader motivates the crew of a boat, and each member of that crew is necessary if the boat is to gain a competitive pace and ultimately emerge as the winner of the race. A leader yelling directions to other leaders will not move a boat; you need the rest of the specialized crew. The stroke, the seven, and the bowman are as important as the leader in a boat. In the case of a business, all crew members are important if the organization is to survive whatever storms are brewing in the marketplace.

My mother was a registered nurse and worked as a hospital administrator for many years. She supervised other health-care workers and support staff after she was promoted to the management team. "Every team member matters" was her motto. I distinctly remember her telling me this as a teenager just when I was entering the workforce. She told me that when she got to work, if the housekeeping staff was cleaning the floors, she always made it a priority to stop and say hello, acknowledging and thanking them for their work. Often, those in lower-status work feel ignored or are overmonitored; ensuring they are made to feel part of the team can change the entire culture of an organization.

In our teachings around leadership, organizational development, organizational psychology, and "emotional intelligence," we often forget to include all members of the team or crew. The above example is simple, but I hope it demonstrates and supports the importance of this key competency for effective management. The housekeeping team of a hospital is owed respect because of what they do to ensure that everyone enjoys the privilege of working in a clean, healthy environment. Their work is important yet may seem invisible. It affects how staff feel when they walk into their office, or when external visitors come to attend a meeting, or even when a potential patient and their family members show interest in services at the hospital.

Yet the work of these crew members may be undervalued simply because other crew members expect their workplace to be clean and are unconcerned with how that is achieved. We often do not consider how it happens that each day our trash disappears from the bin under our desks, or how the dust, mud, or other detritus from the streets is removed and the surfaces are shiny and clean. We only notice this important service when something goes wrong; then we complain to the facility manager, yet we do not thank that manager or their staff normally. But my mother showed by example that you can express gratitude to these key members of the team. By doing this, you'll create an atmosphere of greater appreciation from all levels of crew members. After all, if one crew member puts down their oar, the boat will not sail straight and may end up running into a rock, another boat, or into some other obstruction. If one section or crew member on a boat does not perform their duties, you notice right away. In an office, you will also notice how important other crew members are when they stop pulling their weight. It is far less stressful to value each crew member and notice and praise them when things are going well, rather than have to come up with tactical measures to correct for them if they decide to put their oars down and leave the job.

Studies of work psychology show most employees will stay at an organization because of how they are treated. If they feel respected, despite other company challenges, they will stay. Each employee has value based on their experience with the corporation, as having to train someone new is costly in terms of both time and money. How an individual is treated may be as or more important than salary in determining an individual's loyalty to their workplace. It seems to me that loyalty is so close to having a personal stake in a workplace, that the goal is to have all employees feel proud to be part of an organization. If all crew members see that the leadership team truly sees and respects their individual merit and views everyone as necessary and not merely as replaceable, then you are likely to create a team that pulls together for success. This is as necessary in a paddleboat as it is in a modern company, according to any theory of good management.

You may think getting a service at a hospital should not be based on frontline customer service, but it is. It is why hospitals spend billions on marketing and sharing their expertise, or on competitive messages to attract patients such as announcements that they are best in this treatment or that. The role of every member fits into their business model, and each member is part of the organization's external relations, image, customer service, and staff satisfaction.

When I was a graduate student and had a summer job at a major publishing company, I had an exchange with the vice president of the company that I never forgot. In fact, it is an experience that gave me wisdom that I use within my own organization daily. At the time, I was working at the front desk, answering on average six telephone lines while greeting guests, managing the mail, and doing some light clerical work. One day, I had the additional task of welcoming candidates for a vacant position. I greeted the candidates as they arrived and gave them an application to complete. Once they completed the application, I let the VP know that a candidate was ready for their interview.

After about five or six candidates on that somewhat hectic Monday morning, the VP interrupted me to ask me my opinion of them. I thought it was strange; we had barely had any conversations prior to this event. In fact, until then, virtually the only words we exchanged had been along the lines of "good morning" and "have a good evening." The conversation we had that day and the questions he asked me have stayed with me since.

First, he asked if any of the candidates were late for their appointed interview time slot. He then asked me how long it took each candidate to complete the written application form and if any had taken longer than the others to complete it. And his final question was, "Which candidate was the kindest to you?" He wanted to know if any had attempted to engage me in conversation, or in any other way stuck out as particularly polite or considerate. At the time, I wondered why he was asking me about the candidates when the position they were interviewing for had nothing to do with being a receptionist. But later I understood. And now, twenty-five years after my time in that publishing company, I still remember his questions, and when I walk into a space where there is a receptionist, a secretary, or a security guard, I am always kind and respectful. His questions taught me that these crew members are often the gatekeepers to even the vice president of the company. His respect for my opinion showed his belief that every crew member matters. Even as a receptionist, an entry-level position, he expected future hires to treat me well.

> *"Teamwork is the ability to work together toward a common vision. The ability to direct individual accomplishments toward organizational objectives. It is the fuel that allows common people to attain uncommon results."*
>
> **—Andrew Carnegie**

Being an effective leader has many components, and I don't believe that anyone is perfect or has perfected being a leader or a manager. Those who are managers are not always leaders, and those who lead often do not know how to manage. This is the complexity faced by many business school programs around the world. The programs that train and educate leaders are continuously studying and predicting the best combinations of hard and soft skills that strong leaders and managers will need. Who can be a manager? What skills do they need to have?

Why is it that effective leaders are chosen to be good at big-picture thinking but are often not good at multitasking or struggle to find the key message within the details? To be effective, then, an organization needs to attract crew members who have what may be lacking in other members of the team. It is kind of an equation. By combining the talents of all of its players, organizations can create a team that can get the job done right every time. This means hiring managers who can work well and respect their subordinates as they acknowledge that, without their crew members' unique skills, the boat cannot maintain its speed or continue to travel in the intended direction. Crew members who have that attention to minutiae that their managers may lack are key to crossing the finish line. By creating a team with the true belief that every crew member matters, the hiring departments can build on strengths and allow for weaknesses. Hiring managers must consider that you cannot have success without understanding the part that each crew member plays in the equation that will get them there.

As an executive in the nonprofit sector, I manage staff members who are at the front line, doing work in challenging communities. The individuals we serve are struggling with issues related to chronic health, poverty, limited economic opportunities, and complex public systems that are often unresponsive to their needs. Much of the time the public systems are punitive in nature. It is these crew members, the frontline members that I and the rest of the organization rely on to deliver the services. They are the ones who allow us to be seen as a successful organization.

To me, the front desk team member and the ones who interact with a participant who is in crisis are as important as the fiscal team members who make sure we have the funds to assist that individual and their family. With the demanding needs of the public/ human services sector, we often find individuals who come in with one or two needs, and after a thorough assessment we realize they have five more needs and perhaps some emerging crises besides the one that made them seek our help. As such, there is no way that we could be effective in meeting the needs of the individual with their family members without the support of other organizations who specialize in services that we do not offer. We have come to understand the importance of effective partnerships that are mutually respectful and beneficial to meet the needs of the individuals and families we help. To support individuals and families with a host of diverse needs, we need to collaborate and consider external people as part of our team, crew members who can support the community with us. Together, by looking at the bigger picture and cooperating with a full range of crew members, some internal to our organization and some external, we can best support vulnerable members of the community, leading to their success and to ours. Business leaders know finding collaborators is part of effective leadership. It is the key to successful outcomes.

When I interview potential candidates, particularly those who will be supervisors, I ask them to tell me what they like about supervising people as well as what they do not like. Of course, prospective candidates usually go very lightly when answering this question, as the nature of the relationship is that they are often trying to guess what I am after, rather than answering authentically. They will often be more constructive with their answers, such as finding a way to make what they do not like about supervising demonstrate a positive character trait, afraid that if they admit to not liking an aspect of the job they are applying to, they will not get the job. It makes them twist themselves in knots rather than doing what I'd like: admit that supervising others has its frustrations.

The one thing I know for sure is that the most difficult part of supervising people is people. Employees come to work with diverse experience and expertise, and at the moment you meet them, they may be dealing or managing a challenging set of circumstances in their lives. For example, even if they have a valuable license or degrees that allow them to put letters at the ends of their names, you cannot tell immediately what is going on in their world. As each of the candidates does their best to look like the most confident and competent person there is, internally they may be struggling because they are unsure about how they'll handle childcare if they get the job, maybe their marriage is faltering, or they got hardly any sleep because their newborn was awake all night. This unpredictable part of people management is rarely stated directly as an answer to my question, but this is what I am looking to have them describe. To be a leader of a crew, you must be able to manage both the positive and the negative. If one of your crew members is having a bad day, you ask another to take up some of the slack and lead them all such that the organization still pulls together as one. Every crew member matters, and leaders must support each of them and be able to reach out when they, themselves, need support.

Building a crew from top to bottom is perhaps not

always the best way, but that is typically how it is done. When we create a team, it is usual to begin at the top with the leadership team. I absolutely agree that the leader sets the tone and provides direction and guidance to allow for successfully operating an organization. A lot of time is spent ensuring that the leadership team has a great salary and competitive benefits package so that they want to join the team and feel invested in it, just as the company demonstrates its investment in them through that package. Imagine if, based on the goals and objectives of the very foundation of the organization, we started with the frontline team members, the members who represent your company to those who interact with it. Imagine if we put the same energy into hiring the best receptionist, or the best cleaning person, mailroom clerk, or other so-called lower-tier position, as we did the CEO? What would that mean for organizations? How would that change the way we work collaboratively as a team? This might just be the way to build a team that understands and acknowledges that we all bring some form of expertise to the table that is respected and compensated.

◆　◆　◆

Being able to collaborate as team members is essential to meeting whatever business goal is on the table.

No one can lead alone. The crew cannot follow your leadership if they do not understand your overall goals. Organizations have to invest in training, supporting their staff with not only equitable pay but a benefits package that covers their day-to-day life and needs. Sharing the big picture or amazing idea works only if your crew is on board. If you take care of the leadership team only but are aware that what you have offered to other crew members leaves them unable to meet all the needs of their families, how can they give their full concentration and energy to the job as required? If they cannot focus because you have not provided for their economic and health-based needs fairly, then you have created the conditions that will make your team fail.

The COVID pandemic has changed every aspect of a workplace. With so many more people working remotely, who would have thought we could manage, supervise, and maintain cohesive teams? Yet it is happening, although it is like steering a boat without the crew members physically in the boat. It involves a lot more trust of team members than leaders thought was possible. Leaders desperate to micromanage a dispersed workforce will be stressed beyond their capacity if they stick to the idea that workers slack off if they cannot be seen in their cubicles within an open plan office. They have to give in and trust and respect the integrity of their team. They have to believe that every crew member wants what they want: to win the race. Furthermore, how do we extend the team-building approaches we are used to when our crew members are dispersed around the neighborhood, the state, or even around the country? We are used to controlling the crew within a single building. Leaders have had to let go of older modes of management and simply learn to trust that their crew members have the muscle memory to keep rowing together to maintain their spot in the marketplace.

The COVID pandemic is an example of our need to pay attention to every crew member in society, not only within our organizations. Just as within an organization we may expect things we rely on to run smoothly, such as the coffee and snacks to be available in the cafeteria and the hand dryer to work when we use the rest room, we do the same within society. We often take for granted public servants, bus drivers, emergency service workers, truck drivers, grocery store stockers, and other essential workers who labor invisibly and seamlessly behind the scenes. The pandemic showed us just how much we rely on these crew members. Until we got shaken up by this force we could not control, we often failed to recognize the importance of key crew members in our society.

And now, as the pandemic caused by COVID-19 has shown, the crew may be considered even wider yet. As a leader in a nonprofit that helps the vulnerable within my local community, I know that my community is not safe unless communities like it throughout my state, my country, and even the world are also safe. We will constantly need to maintain this big ship if we want to remain safe ourselves. Every crew member matters in so many contexts. Thus, the challenge of Everybody Paddling continues.

PERSPECTIVE: BELONGING

Dr. Danielle R. Moss, CEO, Oliver Scholars

When I was fifteen, I joined my church's young adult gospel choir. It was one of my favorite activities throughout high school. Although I could carry a tune, I wasn't the best singer, I didn't have the best voice, and because some of the members had professional singing experience, I never sang a solo. But something magical happened every time we sang together. The melodies and harmonies were amazing. We were so good, in fact, that sometimes people would weep when we sang. I enjoyed the choir because, even though I didn't have lots of personal friendships with the other choir members, when we got into those choir stands, I knew I was safe, I knew my participation mattered, I felt seen, I knew I belonged. That powerful sense of belonging to something greater than myself had everything to do with our choir director's leadership, talent, and skill. He had a way of bringing all these different young people with varying degrees of ability together in a way that was magical.

As leaders, we have a unique opportunity to create a similar sense of membership, of belonging in our organizations. When people experience a sense of belonging, they feel accepted, uncompromised, comfortable, connected, safe, visible, valued, and empowered. Acceptance means that my right to hold space in an organization is not questioned. When I feel uncompromised, I don't feel compelled to hide my authentic self for fear of reprisal. When I feel comfortable at work, I can move through my day-to-day interactions with relative ease. When I feel connected at work, I can connect to the experiences and values I share with my colleagues and respect the things that make us different. When I feel safe at work, I do not have to navigate the traps of racism, sexism, and other isms; we are all moving in the same direction with common purpose. When I feel visible, I have clear evidence that my experience and expertise are seen and recognized by my colleagues.

When I feel valued, my contributions are recognized and attributed to me. And, when I feel empowered, I have the latitude and support to help shape, improve, and guide the work of my organization without fear of overstepping positional power.

What does it mean to be a leader who cultivates belonging? First, you've got to get clear about your own values and your personal mission. Who do you want to be in the world? How do you want to show up? How close are you to becoming who you say you are? Who is giving you feedback as a leader? It's hard for us to see ourselves as others experience us. Remember that people often forget what you say, but they do remember how you made them feel. Who are the people on your team or in your organization who feel safe enough, or have enough relationship with you to tell you when you're missing the mark and tell you when you're spot-on? What would it take for you, as a leader, to get comfortable not just giving feedback, but also receiving feedback? Does your organization have protocols for eliciting feedback beyond the traditional 360 instruments some of us may have experience with? Explore some practices for giving and receiving feedback across roles and functions, and explore what it would mean to introduce them into your organization. We can't correct or address what we don't know or can't name.

In a traditional hierarchy, power is concentrated at the top of the organizational chart and is wielded in ways that sometimes keep the folks who are actually driving organizational results guessing about how to position themselves and their work. Moving toward becoming a Belonging Organization requires a reimagining of power, authority, leadership, and accountability. Getting to "belonging" requires a "laying bare" of our own biases, experiences, limitations, and strengths. We've all got back stories—no one comes to work as a blank slate. We are bringing our own lives, memories, and past work experiences with us. Sometimes, those experiences make us better at what we do; they've helped to sharpen the saw. But sometimes, those experiences get in the way of our ability to see and connect with others. What tapes are playing in the background when you're at work? What do you think you know and understand about the people in your organization, and what motivates them?

One of the key enemies of belonging is bias. The stories we bring to the workplace about other people can often undermine the values of belonging. Researchers at Harvard's Project Implicit have discovered that even people from marginalized groups have implicit bias. Having biases is often confirmation that our beliefs about, and attitudes toward, one another are shaped by our families, communities, education, and culture. Biases become dangerous when they influence our behavior in ways that result in harm to others; examples of that harm could be not recruiting from state colleges and universities because you think their students are less prepared than students from private universities, or not inviting women colleagues to off-hours golf outings because you assume they can't play. The list goes on.

The internal stories we've all developed over time about who is capable and who is not, who has value and who does not, and who best reflects workplace norms are really a manifestation of who has power and who does not. For example, "professionalism" in the workplace can solidify the normalization of white male preferences and norms as a standard in the workplace. Cultural expectations in the workplace about what we should wear, how we should speak, how we should communicate, and how we should groom ourselves aka the "uniform of work" are really just manufactured norms by one group with power designed to function as metrics for determining who gets access and who does not. Nothing about performative professionalism has anything to do with actual competence or results. While we are working to confront and dismantle biases that don't serve us, we also need to develop organizational values, practices, and rituals that challenge our biases as we build more equitable leadership habits. This is real work.

When our biases and preferences result in the exclusion of others, we need strategies to unlearn them. Sometimes, the best way to explore belonging in your organization is to ask who is not at the table; who does not have access to certain meetings, projects, opportunities; or who gets to participate in opportunities for formal and informal engagement and who does not. I thought I had the DEI game locked down . . . until a colleague asked me if my organization's website was accessible to the hearing and sight impaired.

As you begin to strive for a culture of belonging, you'll need to ask yourselves what success looks like. Are you hoping to diversity your workforce by 25 percent over the next few years? What does diversity mean for your organization? More women? More people of color? More differently abled people? More progressive benefits for nontraditional families? More LGBTQIA hires? What about management and leadership? What will you be looking for to determine that you're moving the needle? Compensation parity? Promotion parity? How will you hold leaders across the business accountable for getting results? What will accountability look like for the people who undermine your efforts—because change is hard?

How will you reward the people who advance diversity within your organization—to demonstrate that this is a core business priority?

Many organizations hire a lone chief diversity officer then wonder why their people go back to business as usual. These professionals are often hired with a great deal of fanfare but are frequently assigned few staff, limited resources, and ultimately no power—an absolute recipe for ineffectiveness. No matter what your business is, I can tell you this—we spend money on the things we care about. Hire a team to work across the business to help build a culture of belonging from the back office to the leadership ranks. People who are used to having all the power and all the influence and all the access will need coaching and support as they work toward creating a more welcoming and supportive culture to create belonging for an evolving workforce.

Ultimately, there is belonging when people in your organization are thriving. The dictionary defines the verb *thrive* as "to prosper, to grow and develop vigorously, and to be successful." So, what does it really mean? When there is belonging, traditionally underrepresented and marginalized groups don't just exist in our organizations. We have opportunities to be nurtured, developed, and promoted. When there is belonging, everyone who is bringing something meaningful to the table has access to resources and information, meaningful and developmental feedback, mentors and sponsors, the benefit of the doubt, and influence and power. Our lived experiences in organizations are the truest testament to how well you've done. Only those who have been traditionally left at the margins can say whether or not their experiences have improved; the power over progress really must shift to them. Men don't get to tell women that they've done enough to level the playing field or that women are better off. That power, to name their shifting experiences, belongs squarely in the hands of women, just as it belongs to other marginalized groups.

The important thing to remember is that leadership for all is possible. It is possible for leaders to build organizational communities where diverse perspectives, ideas, and contributions can flourish; where workers feel safe to speak their truths, feel safe to show up as themselves, feel supported to participate in building organizational success, feel recognized for their contributions, feel safe to make mistakes, and feel energized by the possibilities that blossom when there is belonging.

CONCLUSION

It's been an interesting journey to this point. By now you've seen how to overcome separate units inside any organization; how to motivate employees through fair, consistent treatment; how to handle complaints; the value of good, transparent communication; and the importance of mission and vision statements and consequent actions.

Following these guidelines, anyone can be an excellent leader, and a team can be built and maintained. However, there's one more aspect to consider: moving away from self-interest and toward serving others. Good managers do not just direct; they also recognize their role as a facilitator, as a role model, and as an instrument for helping others achieve their success.

Motivational speaker Anthony Robbins put the feeling this way: "Only those who have learned the power of sincere and selfless contribution experience life's deepest joy: True Fulfillment."[1]

The problem for all of us, including me, is that for a long time life was simply about *me*. It had to be; remember the quote from Hillel? "If I am not for myself, who will be?" We have all, at various times, focused on achievement and gaining success. Conversations were built around how much *I* wanted to accomplish my career goals, how stressful the whole process was for *me*, how *I* could better *my* chances, and so forth.

It seemed that the only pronouns I was familiar with were *I* and *me*. The more I focused on where I wanted to go, the less I focused on the true purpose that we have on this earth. As time progressed, however, I became open to the possibility of selfless action, which, paradoxically, can be the most self-fulfilling action; it gave me purpose.

More and more, I realize just how selfish we human beings naturally are. All of us have a tendency to be self-centered, even though many of us may not be willing to admit it. In truth, however, leaders have to be able to put themselves second and others first. That's how people get motivated to do their work. My agency provides services twenty-four hours a day; I also have to be available all the time. I have to respect everyone who is contributing, who is paddling alongside me. I have to be flexible and willing to change in order to benefit someone else.

I need to live a life that is centered on serving others, meeting their needs, and giving of myself to accomplish what is best for them. By doing so, I demonstrate the two key traits that every successful leader must embody:

◇ **Kindness.** I have worked under tyrants; maybe you have too. Kindness accomplishes far more.

◇ **Integrity.** This is revealed when no one is looking at you. A leader with integrity is emulated and admired. The end result is that not only do your employees want you to guide them: They are eager to pick up their paddles and join you.

And now we come to the time to act. I have talked about change, but such words have no meaning without some action behind them. We see that happen throughout society; nothing really happens, even as the rhetoric rolls on. We remain stagnant and cannot move.

The solution is to commit to being a better leader. Think of it as a New Year's resolution you really keep.

◇ Act beyond expectations.
◇ Act along with your words.
◇ Act with your voice, all the time.
◇ Act at work, at home, and throughout your community.
◇ Act when no one else is looking.
◇ Act, even if you are the only one.

Now . . . you are ready to pick up your paddle and start moving forward. Others will follow.

DR. CHARLES A. MONTORIO-ARCHER
Esq., MPA, CCEP, CHC, 6S

Charles A. Montorio-Archer is a nonprofit executive with experience founding, growing, and turning around human service organizations through strategic planning, advocacy, operations improvement, financial management, and relationship building. He has extensive expertise in board governance; regulation compliance; policy reform; community outreach; Diversity, Equity, and Inclusion (DEI); and cultural transformation.

Charles is president and chief executive officer of One Hope United (OHU), a multistate nonprofit that creates opportunities for children and families by providing early education, foster care, adoption, counseling, residential, and other support services. Previously, Charles was cofounder and chief executive officer of The Thrive Network, a nonprofit organization that advocates and serves the interests of children, adults, and families with intellectual development disabilities. Charles was also an adjunct professor, School of Public Affairs at Bernard Baruch College, City University of New York.

Charles has been a member of countless boards of directors and appointed to numerous councils and commissions throughout his career. Charles is currently commissioner for Illinois Youth Budget Commission and Illinois Commission on Poverty Elimination and Economic Security. He is also a board member of Illinois Collaboration on Youth, Chicago Alliance for Collaborative Effort, and Florida Coalition for Children, and a member of Casey Family Programs 2020 Race Equity Improvement Collaborative.

Charles earned a Doctor of Philosophy, Public Management and Leadership from Walden University, and a Master of Public Administration from Baruch College/CUNY. He also holds a Juris Doctor from Brooklyn Law School. Charles is a Six Sigma Green and Black Belt, a Certified Health Care Compliance Professional, and a Certified Compliance and Ethics Professional.

Charles is the author of *Everybody Paddles: A Leader's Blueprint to Creating a Unified Team.* He is a frequent speaker and panelist for professional associations, including two TEDx Talks, and is often quoted in the media and industry publications.

347.578.3557 | C.MONTORIOARCHER@ONEHOPEUNITED.ORG
LINKEDIN.COM/IN/CHARLESMONTORIOARCHER

ENDNOTES

Introduction

1 "Rabbi Hillel Quotes," BrainyQuotes, BookRags Media Network (http://www.
   brainyquote.com/quotes/authors/r/rabbi_hillel.html), accessed September 25,
   2013.

2 "History of the Concept of the Individual and Individuality in Western Society,"
   World Academy of Art and Science (http://www.worldacademy.org/forum/history-
   concept-individual-and-individuality-western-society), accessed February 14, 2010.

3 "Donald J. Trump," TweetWood, Manusis Technology (http://tweetwood.com/
   realDonaldTrump/tweet/286912989322424320), accessed September 25, 2013.

Principle One

1 "Yesterday, When I Was Young," performed by Roy Clark, written by Charles
   Aznavour; Lyricsmode; Viacom (http://www.lyricsmode.com/lyrics/r/roy_clark/
   yesterday_when_i_was_young.html), accessed September 25, 2013.

2 B. R. Ambedkar, BrainyQuote, BookRags Media Network (http://www.brainyquote.
   com/quotes/authors/b/b_r_ambedkar.html), accessed September 25, 2013.

3 Ray Williams, "Is Gen Y Becoming the New 'Lost Generation'?" *Psychology Today*,
   April 8, 2013 (http://www.psychologytoday.com/blog/wired-success/201304/
   is-gen-y-becoming-the-new-lost-generation), accessed April 3, 2014.

4   Brian Moore, "The Worst Generation?" *New York Post*, May 10, 2010 (http://
     nypost.com/2010/05/10/the-worst-generation/), accessed April 3, 2014.

5   Tom Rath and James K. Harter, *Wellbeing: The Five Essential Elements* (New York:
     Gallup Press, 2010).

6   "Gallup: 'Managers from Hell' Cost US Between $450 Billion to $550 Billion
     Annually," *Daily Caller*, June 25, 2013 (http://dailycaller.com/2013/06/25/gallup-
     managers-from-hell-cost-us-between-450-billion-to-550-billion-annually/),
     accessed April 3, 2014.

7   Cheryl Snapp Conner, "Mentally Strong People: The 13 Things They Avoid," *Forbes*,
     November 18, 2013 (http://www.forbes.com/sites/cherylsnappconner/2013/11/18/
     mentally-strong-people-the-13-things-they-avoid/), accessed April 3, 2014.

8   Helen Keller, The Quotations Page (http://www.quotationspage.com/quote/3141.
     html), accessed September 25, 2013.

9   *"You've Got to Be Carefully Taught," lyrics by Oscar Hammerstein II, music by Richard*
     Rodgers; copyright ©1949, Oscar Hammerstein II and Richard Rodgers, renewed;
     Williamson Music, owner of publication and allied rights.

10   Bruce Piasecki, *Doing More with Teams: The New Way to Winning* (Hoboken, NJ:
     Wiley, 2013).

Principle Two

1   Martin Luther King Jr., BrainyQuote, BookRags Media Network (http://www.
     brainyquote.com/quotes/quotes/m/martinluth105087.html), accessed April 3,
     2014.

2   "Company Fortune 500," Missionstatements.com (http://www.missionstatements.
     com/fortune_500_mission_statements.html), accessed September 25, 2013.

3   James C. Collins and Jerry I. Porras, "Building Your Company's Vision," *Harvard*
     Business Review (http://hbr.org/1996/09/building-your-companys-vision),
     accessed September 25, 2013.

Principle Three

1   Gallup survey cited in Timothy Egan, "Checking Out," *New York Times*, June
     20, 2013 (http://opinionator.blogs.nytimes.com/2013/06/20/checking-out/?_
     php=true&_type=blogs&_r=0), accessed April 4, 2014.

2   Smith cited in Patrick M. Kelley, "How to Identify and Deal with Whining
    Cry Baby (WCB)," LA Sheriff's Organization (http://la-sheriff.org/divisions/
    leadership-training-div/bureaus/dli/assets/dluarticles-kelly.pdf), accessed
    September 25, 2013.

3   Martin Luther King Jr., "Rediscovering Lost Values," The Martin Luther
    King Jr. Papers Project, Stanford University (http://mlk-kppo1.stanford.edu/
    primarydocuments/Vol2/540228RediscoveringLostValues.pdf), accessed
    September 25, 2013.

4   Judith Wright and Bob Wright, *Heart of the Fight* (Oakland, CA: New Harbinger
    Publications, 2016).

Principle Four

1   "Pick Yourself Up," written by Jerome Kern and Dorothy Fields, performed by
    Frank Sinatra; copyright © T. B. Harms, Shapiro Bernstein & Co, Inc., Aldi
    Music.

2   Alex "Sandy" Pendleton, "The Hard Science of Teamwork," March 20, 2012
    (http://blogs.hbr.org/2012/03/the-new-science-of-building-gr/), accessed April 11,
    2014.

3   Janine Driver, "The Power of Subliminal Communication," September 23, 2011
    (http://www.doctoroz.com/blog/janine-driver/power-subliminal-communication),
    accessed April 3, 2014.

4   Julius Fast, *Body Language* (New York: Simon & Schuster, 1970).

5   Cited in Jay Yarow, "Larry Ellison Made Steve Jobs Fall Out of His Seat Laughing
    When He Told Him This Story," *Business Insider* (http://www.businessinsider.
    com/gil-amelio-steve-jobs-2011-10), accessed September 25, 2013.

6   B. Moté & S. C. Knight, "Leading with Dignity: One Organization's Story of
    Building Resiliency Through Service to Others." ZERO TO THREE 41, no. 4
    (June 6, 2021), https://www.zerotothree.org/resources/4067-leading-with-dignity-
    one-organization-s-story-of-building-resiliency-through-service-to-others.

Principle Five

1   Fierce, Inc., survey cited in Phaedra Brotherton, "More Employee Input and
    Accountability Yield More Effective Practices," American Society for Training

and Development (http://www.astd.org/Publications/Magazines/TD/TD-Archive/2012/05/Intelligence-MoreEmployee-Input-and-Accountability-Yield-More-Effective-Practices), accessed September 25, 2013.

2   Greenberg cited in Tim Donnelly, "How to Get Feedback from Employees," in Inc. (http://www.inc.com/guides/2010/08/how-to-getfeedback-from-employees.html), accessed September 25, 2013.

3   Carnegie cited in "Andrew Carnegie Quotes," GoodReads, Inc. (http://www.goodreads.com/quotes/251192teamwork-is-the-ability-to-work-together-towards-a-common), accessed September 25, 2013.

Conclusion

1   Anthony Robbins, cited in tonyrobbins.com (http://www.tonyrobbins.com/resources/ pdfs/2012-Platinum-Partners-Brochure.pdf), accessed September 25, 2013.